LOUISIANA PLANTATIONS: REAL TO REEL

LOUISIANA PLANTATIONS: REAL TO REEL

By
Ed and Susan Poole

Learn About Network, L.L.C.

Louisiana Plantations: Real to Reel

PUBLISHED BY:

Learn About Network, L.L.C.
P. O. Box 3181
Harvey, LA 70059
(504) 298-5267

First edition published 2014

ISBN: 978-0-9815695-8-1

IMAGES

All images of movie stills and posters featured in this book are from the private collection of the authors.

ADDITIONAL COPIES

Additional copies of this publication may be ordered through HollywoodOnTheBayou.com.

TABLE OF CONTENTS

Ed and Susan Poole
Film Accessory Researchers

For over 35 years Ed and Susan Poole have been involved with documenting, recording and preserving film accessories (i.e., press books, movie stills, movie posters, general press materials, etc.). Their path has evolved from being just collectors to retail and wholesale dealers and eventually to full time researchers.

Their accomplishments on a national and international level include:

- **Published the** first reference book on movie posters, *Collecting Movie Posters*, released in 1997 by McFarland Publishers.

- Published 16 additional reference books including: *Learn About Movie Posters; Learn About International Movie Posters; Movie Still Identification Book; Legality of U.S. Movie Posters; Movie Trailer Identification Codes; National Screen Service Accessory Codes; Hollywood On The Bayou and Louisiana Film History*.

- In 2001, developed the first reference website on movie posters designed for novice to intermediate level collectors: LearnAboutMoviePosters.com.

- In 2005, developed the first cross referenced research film accessory database with 100,000 images online: MoviePosterDataBase.com.

- In 2009, developed the first advance research website for documenting press still codes, lithographer plate numbers, etc. - GlobalCinemaResearch.org.

In 2010, the Pooles realized that documentation of local film history was basically non-existent. The Pooles are firm believers that the research and documentation of this history is a necessary foundation for development of many associated industries such as tourism and education.

The Pooles are on a quest to BUILD that foundation through:

Books: In 2011, to establish a starting foundation, the Pooles used their research to create ***Hollywood On The Bayou***, documenting 1170 films made in or about Louisiana. They then went to work on local background stories and filming locations. The following year, Margaret Media published a combination of stories AND the Hollywood On The Bayou book to create ***Louisiana Film History: A Comprehensive Overview Beginning 1896.*** Since that time, the Pooles have produced two other books: ***Crescent City Cinema Movie Posters*** and ***Heroine to Hussy: Women in Louisiana Films.***

Exhibits: In February 2012, the first exhibit on Louisiana Film History was opened at Ellender Memorial Library at Nicholls State University and ran for 4 months during their Jubilee. Since that time, work is being done on smaller more flexible exhibits that include storyboards interspersed with original movie posters and stills. These can be circulated around the state for short periods of time and smaller space allocations. This is to present to the public the massive amount of filming that has taken place throughout the state for over 115 years.

Film Prints: Some of the most iconic films ever put on the screen have been made in Louisiana. The Pooles have recreated over 50 vintage movie posters on 12"x18" glossy card stock. These are professionally printed and made available to "friends" organizations and fund raising groups to bring more awareness to Louisiana's wonderful film history and to help fund expansion projects to a wider area. All posters can be seen in the Print Shop on the website.

Lectures/Presentations: Two different Powerpoint presentations are available on Louisiana Film History. Both include clips of vintage film trailers, newspaper clippings and behind the scenes stories. One is ½ hour for luncheons and groups outside the film industry and the other is a full hour that includes a lot more details on a wider variety of films. Also available is a workshop on collecting film accessories (movie posters, stills, pressbooks) for film fests; an exclusive 7 minute documentary on Vitascope Hall (the first seated indoor theater in the U.S. opened in New Orleans in 1896), Louisiana trailers and silent films which can be used as backgrounds for special events, etc.

Research: Expansion of research information on ALL films made in or about Louisiana is being created and compiled to be available for research students, film makers, industry professionals and the general public.

Websites: HollywoodOnTheBayou.com is now open and has over 50 vintage Louisiana trailers and lists of Louisiana films by time period AND by Parish. This will be expanded to include Louisiana people in film and Louisiana film studios. An entry page for libraries is currently being created to expand access to vital information through a wider variety of education facilities to help expand availability.

ABOUT THIS BOOK

Louisiana has been a favorite shooting location for filmmakers for almost 130 years. As early as 1898, the largest movie studio of the time, American Mutoscope and Biograph Company, came to the state to film actuals of New Orleans and the surrounding areas. For the next thirteen decades, movie makers have continued to come to Louisiana.

Why does Louisiana peak the interests of film producers? There are a number of reasons. Two of the major draws are the colorful history and the magnificent architecture. These two factors are clearly evident Louisiana's famous -- and infamous -- plantations.

The plantations of Louisiana represent a period in history from the birth of our great nation to a time when it was nearly torn apart. They capture the heart, soul and spirit of the people who inhabited them, from the affluent to the poor. The land, homes and buildings tell the story of the great planters of cotton, sugar, indigo before the Civil War and how they built their empires on the backs of slaves. Many stood as witnesses to the wrath of war, and many suffered near destruction.

Fortunately many of these gems have survived through the efforts of individuals who spent time and money to restore them to their old glory. These living monuments offer visitors a chance to relive a time in our country's early history. They also provide a unique filming opportunity for movie makers.

In the "reel" world, these plantations have been used as backdrops for time periods as early as the antebellum era to today. They have been used to tell tales of the Civil War; they have served as the home for the rich, famous and political of all time periods; their "ghostly" reputations provide an excellent atmosphere for films dealing with the "other world"; and can represent any house in the USA.

Louisiana's Plantations: Real to Reel features 38 plantations located around the state of Louisiana. It focuses on their rich history and how filmmakers from around the world have used them to make their movie magic.

The plantations are presented alphabetically. Following a brief "real" history of the plantation is a listing of the movies filmed there. Each movie title has a brief synopsis along with cast, director and filming information.

There are several instances where a film was shot at multiple locations. In this case, the movie synopsis will appear on only one plantation. However, a notation will be provided for each plantation that was a part of the film.

AFTON VILLA PLANTATION
St. Francisville, Louisiana

The original owner of Afton Gardens, John Crocker, built an eight-room house on 15,000 acres of land in 1790. David Barrow and his first wife Sarah were given this house and land as a marriage gift from his father Bartholomew Barrow in the 1820s. After Sarah Barrow died in 1846, David married his second wife Susan Woolfolk.

Susan was not impressed with their modest two-story residence. Barrow agreed that she could build any house she wanted as long as the original dwelling remained intact. Susan agreed by building over and around the original, smaller residence. Thus, began the creation of Afton Villa and its splendid gardens.

Impressed by the fashionable Gothic mansions she had seen in France and along the Hudson River, Mrs. Barrow decided upon a Gothic revival home. Construction of the splendid towered and turreted French residence began in 1849 and took eight years to complete. The L-shaped house with forty rooms, including fifteen bedrooms, was one of the largest and most unusual plantation homes in Louisiana.

The stucco exterior contained insert porches, balcony porches, stem pillars, mouldings, panels, and panel tracery - all carved out of logs - piece by piece. Inside the home, the stair hall was comparable with any English manor of the period. Carved doors, spindles, casings, and mouldings were completed with Gothic accuracy. English interpretation was the predominating detail of the house - with a reverse curve bordering on late flamboyant, a French interpretation.

The Barrows lived at Afton through the Civil War. Following David Barrow's death in 1874, Mrs. Barrow left the plantation, never returning. She is buried in her native Kentucky.

The house served as a finishing school for girls at one time and was even abandoned for several years.

In 1915, Dr. Robert E. Lewis of Illinois bought Afton Villa, and with his wife, made the outstanding contribution of resurrecting the old gardens. The last owners of this mansion, Mr. and Mrs. Wallace Percy, purchased the property in 1945 and completely restored the house to its former grandeur. Mrs. Percy purchased as much of the original furniture as she could find as well. The mansion was destroyed by fire in 1963.

The property was sold in 1972 to Genevieve and Morrell Trimble who embarked on a huge 20-year project to restore the lost gardens. They turned the pool house into living quarters. Afton Villa Gardens is open to the public.

The gardens were featured in the 2010 film *Loss of a Teardrop Diamond* (below).

Loss of a Teardrop Diamond - 2010

See St. Louis Plantation.

ALBANIA PLANTATION
Jeanerette, Louisiana

Listed on the National Register of Historic Places, the Albania Plantation is a 12,000 sq. ft three story elegant Greek Revival home located along the Bayou Teche, just outside the town of Jeanerette, Louisiana. It was built by Charles Francois Grevemberg, a German immigrant who arrived in Louisiana around 1792. He married Euphemie Fuselier, a French Royalist refugee in 1915. Seventeen years later, he was granted land from Louis XVI and Napoleon I.

Grevemberg (right) built Albania in stages between 1837 and 1842. It has two front entrances, one facing the former Spanish Trail and the other facing the Bayou Teche. The two distinct facades ensured that Grevemberg could receive guests who arrived via carriage or bayou.

After Grevemberg's death, Euphemie and her son Charles continued to manage Albania. Records of the sugar crops made in Louisiana 1859-1860 show Mrs. Grevemberg producing 475 hogsheads of sugar on the Bayou Teche. By 1860, Euphemie and her son owned a total of 280 slaves, 1,507 acres of improved land, and 5,000 acres of unimproved land. Albania remained in the hands of the Grevemberg family until 1885, when they had to sell the house due to defaulting on their debts.

Isaac Delgado, a New Orleans sugar planter and banker, acquired the Albania plantation after foreclosing on the mortgage. The Jamaican born Delgado immigrated to the United States at age 14. He worked with his uncle Samuel in the family's sugar brokerage firm. After Samuel's death, Isaac took over the company.

After buying Albania, he continued working the land although he never actually lived in the house. He sent manager Alan Allain to rebuild the plantation and update its sugar refining equipment. The plantation continued to operate at a profit for many years. After his death, he bequeathed the plantation and its land to the City of New Orleans with the stipulation that the revenues go to the Delgado Trades School. The city created the Delgado Albania Plantation Commission to oversee the operation of the plantation.

In 1957, with the house in need of costly repairs, the City of New Orleans sold the plantation house and 10 surrounding acres at public auction. It was acquired by Emily Cyr Bridges, who restored Albania and opened it to the public showcasing her well-known collection. Miss Emily, as she was known, was an enthusiastic antiquarian who traveled the countryside seeking and purchasing Southern plantation furniture and Acadian artifacts.

Miss Emily was the daughter of Paul N. Cyr, who served as Lieutenant Governor of Louisiana from 1928 to 1931 under Governor Huey Long. Long and Cyr would soon become political rivals, with Cyr trying twice to declare himself governor of the state. In one incident, when Long was elected to the U.S. Senate, Cyr had himself sworn in as governor claiming that Long had vacated the office. Long had the National Guard and State Police bar Cyr from the Governor's Mansion. Because of the bad blood between Cyr and Long, Emily banned Long's name from being spoken at Albania.

Emily was an accomplished woman in her own right. She was a pioneer aviator who flew patrol missions over the Louisiana coast as a member of the Civil Air Patrol during World War II. When her husband James Bridges died in 1968 in an accident, Emily's interest waned and Albania slipped once again into disrepair. She died in 2003.

In 2004, the rundown plantation was purchased by New York painter Hunt Slonem, who fell in love with Louisiana's architecture in the 1970's while attending Tulane University. At the time of purchase, all of the home's contents, which included over 50 years worth of Bridges family artwork, antiques and curiosities, had been auctioned off.

Once renovations started, the producers of the 2006 film **All the King's Men** approached Slonem about filming at Albania, providing the new owner with additional monies to fund further restorations.

In addition to **All the king's Men**, the 2009 film **In the Electric Mist** was also shot on location at the Albania Plantation.

All the King's Men - 2006

Steven Zaillian directed this version of Robert Penn Warren's classic political novel which featured Sean Penn in the iconic role of Willie Stark. The film also starred Jude Law, Kate Winslet, James Gandolfini, Mark Ruffalo and New Orleans born Patricia Clarkson. Louisiana's Robert Carville served as the film's executive producer.

The photo above features Sean Penn and director Steven Zaillian discussing a scene in **All the Kings Men**, 2006.

All the Kings Men tells the story of a populist southern politician whose ambitious nature sets him up for corruption and scandal. Stark's character is often thought to be inspired by the life of Huey P. Long, former Louisiana governor and U.S. senator in the mid-1930s. Huey Long was at the height of his career when he was assassinated in 1935; just a year earlier, Robert Penn Warren had begun teaching at Louisiana State University.

Willie Stark is a man of the people, and for the people, at least that's what he tells the people. Propelled into a race for governor by opposing forces looking to split the "hick vote," Stark is convinced to not kowtow to the powers that be. His rhetoric grows fiery, and he makes his way into office on a not-so-solid foundation of social-service promises. When idealism gives way to the harsh realities of the time, however, the fast-talking politician is quick to discover just how far one can fall when ambition and power lead to betrayal of one's original motivations. Stark, like Long, is shot to death in the state capitol building by a physician.

While scouting for shooting locations, Patrizia von Brandenstein, the film's production designer, discovered the Albania Plantation. In an interview with *InStyle Home Magazine*, von Brandenstein explained her first impression of Albania. "We stopped the car. I could barely discern something through the thickness of the leaves. And I thought, My God, this is it."

In the film, the Albania Plantation would serve as the Stanton Home, with portions of the main parlor, dining room, kitchen and bedroom, as well as the exteriors, being used. The front entrance facing the Bayou Teche was ideal for the scene where Jude Law arrives by water.

In addition to Albania, other Louisiana shooting locations included the State Capitol in Baton Rouge, the Livingston Parish Fairgrounds, and various sites in Morgan City and New Orleans.

The World Premiere of the film took place at Tulane University's McAlister Auditorium in New Orleans.

In the Electric Mist - 2009

In the Electric Mist is an American-French film based on the novel *In the Electric Mist with Confederate Dead*. It is one of the many books written by James Lee Burke which features the character of Dave Robicheaux, a New Iberia Sheriff's Deputy. This film, which was helmed by French director Bertrand Tavernier (see photo on next page), is set in New Iberia, the home town of Burke.

Tommy Lee Jones plays the character of Robicheaux, a former New Orleans police officer and recovering alcoholic whose demons stem from his service in the Vietnam War; his impoverished childhood in rural Louisiana; his mother's abandonment and subsequent murder; and the death of his father.

In this instance, Robicheaux is soon faced with not one but two murder investigations. Shortly after a film crew arrives to produce a Civil War film, a local prostitute is found murdered. Robicheaux's investigation leads him to a New Orleans mobster who is co-producing the film. At the same time, a second corpse is found in the Atchafalaya Swamp near the movie set. Robicheaux believes the body is the remains of a black man that he saw murdered 35 years earlier.

Bertrand Tavernier behind the camera.

The film also stars local favorite John Goodman, Peter Sarsgaard, Mary Steenburgen, and Ned Beatty.

To ensure the natural and cultural integrity of the book, *In the Electric Mist* was shot on location at Albania Plantation (below), downtown New Iberia, St. Martinville, and surrounding areas along the West Atchafalaya Basin from Catahoula to Charenton . A few of the scenes were shot in post-Katrina New Orleans, which adds to the current feel of the film.

In the Electric Mist was released in two distinct versions due to a conflict between director Tavernier and both his American producer, Michael Fitzgerald, and editor, Roberto Silvi, concerning the cutting of the movie. One of these, 117 minutes long, was shown at the Berlin Film Festival in February 2009 before being released in European cinemas two months later. (See original movie poster below). At the same time, the second version, which was cut very differently from the European version and included different scenes, premiered in New Iberia and was then released straight to DVD.

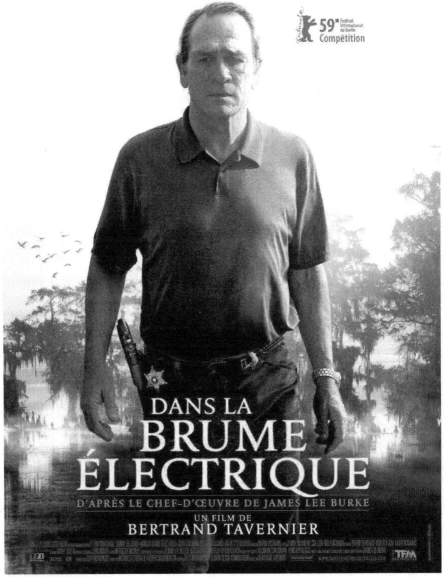

ARDOYNE PLANTATION
Schriever, Louisiana

Ardoyne house is set in a cluster of live oaks on little Bayou Black. The land was purchased by Louisiana state senator, John Dalton Shaffer, son of a noted Terrebonne planter, in 1888. After telling his wife he would build her a "cottage," Shaffer had the 21-room mansion constructed during her absence. It was designed by the New Orleans architectural firm of W. C. Williams and Bros. The cypress and pine used for construction was cut on the property and then properly milled in St. Louis before coming back to Terrebonne as completed features for the house. Ardoyne was built – and named – for a Scottish castle. The name, translated from the Scottish Gaelic, means "little knoll."

Ardoyne contains twenty-one rooms including seven bedrooms, four bathrooms and twelve fireplaces. The first floor boasts sixteen foot cove-molded pine ceilings with octagonal patterns of beaded beams.   It operated as the center of the sugarcane plantation. Migrant workers of German, Italian and African decent were the main workforce of the land and would receive plantation tokens as pay. This plantation is one of the first post Civil War operations and is an example of how the South transitioned from slavery to the Industrial Revolution.

Members of the Shaffer family are still involved with the sugarcane industry today. While Ardoyne did not witness the tragedies related to slavery, the war that ended it or the reconstruction that followed, there were difficulties nonetheless. In 1906 the first recorded case of yellow fever related to what became a widespread outbreak in Terrebonne was at Ardoyne. The Shaffer family, one of the original families of Terrebonne Parish, has owned the home since its construction. This home is on the National Register of Historic Places.

Ardoyne Plantation has been featured in three movies.

Crazy in Alabama - 1999

Ardoyne Plantation was Dove's undertaking parlor (see Magnolia Plantation).

Deadline - 2009

When a screenwriter needs to complete a screenplay, she accepts an offer by a producer friend to stay at a Victorian home he recently purchased. In order to focus on her project, she decides to stay in the home alone. A series of strange occurrences in the house ultimately lead her to a psychological breakdown. This direct-to-video psychological thriller was directed by Sean McConville and starred Brittany Murphy, Thora Birch and Tammy Blanchard.

Ardoyne Plantation served as the Victorian home.

The Tribute - 2009

Tribute, a/k/a Nora Roberts' Tribute, is a 2009 television film directed by Martha Coolidge and starred Brittany Murphy, Jason Lewis, Tippi Hedren and Martha Coolidge.

It follows the story of a former child star who has found happiness in restoring old houses. When she buys her grandmother's Virginia farmhouse, she begins to have haunting dreams of her famous grandmother, who died of an alleged overdose in the house more than 30 years ago. She begins a romantic relationship with her neighbor, who ultimately comforts and protects her when her dark dreams and family secrets turn into a real-life nightmare.

The Tribute was filmed on location at Ardoyne Plantation.

Photo above is a scene from the film featuring Lewis and Murphy in front of Ardoyne.

ASHLAND BELLE HELENE PLANTATION
Ascension Parish, Louisiana

Duncan F. Kenner (left) built Ashland (later named Ashland Belle Helene) for his wife, Anne Guillemine Nanine Bringier, a member of an old and influential French family of Louisiana. Kenner was a sugar planter, horse breeder, lawyer and political figure during the antebellum period. The walls of Ashland (as the Kenner plantation was then known) were adorned with paintings of horses, and the grounds included a racetrack. Kenner himself was a keen advocate of scientific methods of farming and experimented with innovations in the sugar production industry. Kenner is said to have been the first in the state to use the portable railroad to carry cane from fields to mill.

Construction on the mansion began in 1839 and was completed in 1841. Ashland is representative of the massiveness, simplicity, and dignity which are generally held to epitomize the Classical Revival style of architecture. The sixty foot square two story mansion has 28 columns that are three foot square, and thirty-five foot high.

Twelve foot wide galleries wrap around the building on both floors. The building had eight Italian marble fireplaces that were destroyed by vandals in 1959. With its broad spread of eight giant pillars across each facade and its heavy entablature, Ashland is among the grandest and largest plantation houses ever built in the state. Free of service attachments and with a loggia on all four facades, it is a more complete classical statement than the vast majority of Louisiana plantation houses.

When Kenner returned to Ashland at the end of the Civil War, he found his plantation in ruins and his slaves freed, the place having been raided by Union troops in 1862. At the age of 52 he had to start over again, but by persistence and great business skill, and by re-employing as laborers the slaves that had been freed, he built up an estate. When Duncan Kenner died, his plantation was even larger and more valuable than it had been before the war.

In 1889, Ashland was purchased by John B. Reuss, a German immigrant who became a prosperous sugar planter. Reuss re-named the plantation "Belle Helene" in honor of his granddaughter Helene, who later married W.C. Hayward, Sr. From 1939 to 1946 the mansion was unoccupied and unattended until the Hayward family began a major restoration in 1946. By 1959, the grounds were empty again and subject to vandalism.

Shell Oil Company purchased the estate, along with102 acres, from the Hayward family in 1992. They restored the exterior to the original colors, and replaced the roof for preservation in 1997. Excavations were done in 1989, and again in 1992. Evidence of the sugarhouse, 18 cabins, an overseer's house, a blacksmith shop, and other buildings were examined.

Ashland Belle Helene was featured in a number of theatrical and made-for-TV movies.

Little Foxes - **1941**

The Little Foxes was based on the play written by New Orleans native Lillian Hellman. In the film, Bette Davis (right) plays the mincing matriarch of an aristocratic Southern family who stops at nothing to get the money she wants to build a cotton mill in 1900.

When her dying husband refuses to give her money for a surefire business deal with her brothers, her nephew - in cahoots with her brothers - steals $75,000 worth of bonds from her husband so that the deal can be put through. When Regina finds out what they've done, she blackmails them into giving her two thirds of the profits. In order to get her hands on her husband's money, she causes his death by refusing to give him medicine when he suffers a heart attack.

The film also starred Teresa Wright, Herbert Marshall, Patricia Collinge, Dan Duryea and Charles Dingle. It was directed by William Wyler. It opens with the following quotation from *The Song of Solomon* . II.15: "Take us the foxes, the little foxes that spoil the vines; For our vines have tender grapes." The following written prologue then appears onscreen: "Little foxes have lived in all times, in all places. This family happened to live in the deep South in the year 1900."

The above photo shows William Wyler giving directions to Teresa Wright (l) and Bette Davis (r).

This was the third film in which Wyler directed Bette Davis. During filming of *Jezebel* in 1938, rumors swirled that Wyler and Davis were involved in an affair. By the time of the filming of **Little Foxes**, they fought continuously on set about everything from her appearance to the set design.

To capture the southern atmosphere of the film, backgrounds were shot on location at the Belle Helene plantation.

Band of Angels - 1957

See The Cottage - Baton Rouge,

The Beguiled - 1971

The Beguiled tells the story of a dying Yankee soldier at the end of the Civil War in the deep south. Clint Eastwood plays John, a soldier who is rescued by a twelve-year-old girl from a nearby Louisiana boarding school. She manages to get him back to the school, causing immediate alarm to the all-female staff. However, as John recovers, he begins to charm the girls, becoming the object of their awakening sexuality and jealousy runs rampant.

After he rejects the headmistress (Geraldine Page) of the school for a younger girl, John falls down the stairs breaking his leg, which eventually must be amputated. John begins to drink, and his behavior alienates both teachers and students. He makes an attempt to reform, but it is too late, as the headmistress and girls have decided to solve their problem by feeding him poison mushrooms.

The film was based on the book *The Beguiled* by Thomas Cullinan and was directed by Don Siegel. The photo on the right shows Eastwood and Siegel during a rehearsal on set.

The *Exhibitor magazine* review reported that Universal made "a number of cuts" to the film, noting in particular the gory amputation scene, which was cut after the preview audience expressed discomfort with it.

Louisiana's Ashland Belle Helene Plantation served as the boarding school for the film. Modern sources state that Universal wanted Siegel to shoot the film at Disney Studios' Southern plantation lot, but Siegel convinced them that it was cheaper to shoot in Louisiana.

During the making of this film, Clint Eastwood directed his very first film, a behind the scenes look at his director Don Siegel. The documentary, which has a running time of 12 minutes, was titled *The Beguiled, The Storyteller*.

Autobiography of Miss Jane Pittman - 1974

See The Cottage - West Feliciana.

Mandingo - 1975

Mandingo begins in the 1840's on a run-down slave breeding plantation lorded over by Warren Maxwell and his son Hammond. Maxwell insists that Hammond, who is busy bedding the slaves he buys, marry a white woman and father him a son. Hammond travels to New Orleans where he picks up a wife, Blanche, a "bed wench," Ellen, and a Mandingo slave, Mede, whom he trains to be a bare-knuckle fighting champion. The film is based on the novel of the same name by Kyle Onstott. The film stars James Mason, Perry King (below), Susan George, Richard Ward, Brenda Sykes and boxing legend Ken Norton (below) as Mede. It was directed by Richard Fleischer.

Edwin W. Edwards (Governor of Louisiana at the time) was cast as a gambler in the film. According to a *Times Picayune* article that appeared on September 6, 1974, when Edwards was told he would be a gambling dandy, Edwards quipped, "I can handle that." He said he "hustled" for some time to get the movie shot in the state and that it was agreed he would do a small part as a favor to the producers. He shot several scenes but they were removed before release. Upon the advice of public relations staff, Edwards decided the potential damage to his public image when the salacious content of the film was revealed would be too great.

Mandingo was filmed on location in Louisiana. The Ashland Belle Helene Plantation subbed for Falconhurst, the slave breeding plantation of the film's protagonists. Scenes were also filmed at Houmas House Plantation in Burnside and the French Quarter of New Orleans.

Long, Hot Summer - 1985

See The Myrtles

Dark Heritage - 1989

Dark Heritage is an unofficial adaptation of H.P. Lovecraft's "The Lurking Fear." It is the tale of a nameless narrator, a self-described "connoisseur in horrors" who investigates the local tales of a murderous apparition that appears in and around a deserted mansion. After a violent thunderstorm, 30 mutilated bodies are found at a Louisiana campground. Determined to solve the crimes, an investigative reporter and two others go to the deserted mansion of the Dansen clan. They soon uncover a dark local legend about the house and the reclusive Dansens, who may be connected with the murders.

Dark Heritage was a largely amateur production, shot in 1989 by director David McCormick on a very low budget.

The film starred Mark LaCour, Tim Verkaik, Eddie Moore and Joan Parmelee. It was released straight to video.

Ashland Belle Helene served as the deserted Dansen family mansion.

Fletch Lives - 1989

Chevy Chase (below) recreates his role of Irvin "Fletch" Fletcher, a reporter for a Los Angeles newspaper who behaves more like a detective. When he inherits the Bell Isle, a sprawling 80-acre Louisiana plantation from an obscure relative, he quits his job at the paper and takes off to live like a king.

Arriving in Louisiana, he soon discovers that the mansion is run-down and in desperate need of repairs. Trouble begins when a lovely attorney mysteriously turns up dead, a neighborly lawyer warns him to leave town and a ravishing real estate agent comes calling with a persistent offer he may not be able to refuse. Fletch must unravel the reason for the mad land scramble with his trademark bag of hilarious disguises.

The film also stars Hal Holbrook, Julianne Phillips (below) and Cleavon Little.

It was directed by Michael Ritchie (see below).

Ashland Belle Helene served as the plantation home inherited by Fletch. The film also contained scenes shot at Houmas House as well as locations in and around New Orleans, and Thibodaux. The scene below featuring Ashland Belle Helene appeared in Fletch's dream sequence.

ASPHODEL PLANTATION
Jackson, Louisiana

Asphodel Plantation was established in 1820 by Benjamin and Carolyn Kendrick who had migrated to Louisiana from North Carolina. They acquired the 5000 acre property through a Spanish land grant. Benjamin Kendrick began construction of the current home around 1820 as a gift to his wife Caroline. Asphodel was named by the Kendricks after the Greek word for daffodil, a flower which grows readily on the plantation.

The building of the home continued over a ten year period. The main house at Asphodel Plantation is one of Louisiana's finest examples of antebellum architecture. It is an American Greek Revival with a strong Louisiana colonial influence.

During this time, the famous American naturalist and painter of wildlife John James Audubon lived at neighboring Oakley plantation during the 1820's. To support himself while painting, Audubon tutored the children of local plantation owners, including Isabella Kendrick, daughter of Benjamin and Carolyn. While the children typically traveled to Oakley for Audubon's lessons, he often visited Asphodel to personally teach Isabella. It is believed that a number of his paintings were based on sketches done while at Asphodel.

The year that construction of Asphodel was completed, Benjamin Kendrick died, leaving the property to Isabella. She married Colonel David Jones Fluker (right) in 1834. The Flukers were responsible for the final additions to the main house. No further significant changes were made to the house, and what stands today is as Isabel lived in it.

The major crop at Asphodel was cotton. The combination of Asphodel's highly productive land and excellent access to transportation to major cotton markets in Europe and the eastern United States allowed Asphodel to become a very profitable plantation. In the pre-civil war years of 1840 to 1863, more than half the U. S. millionaires were living between Natchez, Mississippi and New Orleans.

In 1854, David died leaving Isabella a widow with twelve children. The Civil War changed the life style of the Flukers, as it did many other southerners. During the Battle of Port Hudson, a group of Union soldiers set fire to Asphodel while Isabella and her children hid in the library. Because so little wood was used in the building of the home, the mostly stone structure put out the fire before any significant damage could be done.

After the war, there were many years of poverty. Katherine and Sarah Smith, descendents of the original owners, came into ownership. For approximately 40 years until their deaths in 1945 and 1948, they never left the grounds. When they died, they were buried in the family plot on the grounds.

Following the death of the Smith sisters, the house was unoccupied until Mr. and Mrs. John Fetzer purchased it in 1948. They completed a restoration of the home in 1953. In 1958, Mr. and Mrs. Robert E. Couhig bought the house and a relative, Mrs. E. B. Briggs, Jr. then owned the home until 1999.

Between 1998-1999, the house went through a total restoration, including adding the two guest houses and the pool house. A new four car garage was built adjacent to the house. Dr. Michael L. Israel, an avid bug and book collector originally from New York, purchased Asphodel Plantation in 2000. He received his PhD from LSU in Entomology.

Recently, Jake and Jodie Seal have transformed the old Asphodel Plantation into a first-rate film studio known as Plantation Village Studios.

The Asphodel cemetery is the only private residential cemetery in Louisiana listed on the National Historic Register. Established in the 1830's with the entombment of Benjamin and Carolyn Kendrick, the cemetery contains the remains of every deceased owner of Asphodel. Asphodel's cemetery has been listed on the National Register's List of Historic Burial Sites."

Asphodel Plantation has attracted a number of filmmakers who chose the area as a background for their films. The following are movies shot on location, either wholly or partially, at Asphodel.

Long, Hot Summer - 1958

See Ramsey Plantation.

Desire in the Dust - 1960

See Oakley Plantation.

Alvarez Kelly - 1966

See Lakeview/Fairview Plantation

Sounder - 1972

Sounder tells the story of a family of African American sharecroppers in rural Louisiana during the Great Depression. The family must regroup to survive after the father is sent to jail for stealing food to feed his family. The title Sounder is the name given to the dog featured in the story.

The cast included Cicely Tyson, Paul Winfield, Kevin Hooks, Eric Hooks, Carmen Matthews and Taj Mahal (below). The film was directed by Martin Ritt.

According to various news sources, the filmmakers originally intended to shoot in Macon, Georgia, but racial tensions caused them to move to Louisiana. In addition to filming at Asphodel, location shooting was also done in areas in East Feliciana and St. Helena parishes near the town of Clinton and Baton Rouge.

Blaze - 1989

This movie tells the story of the latter years of Earl Long, flamboyant governor of Louisiana. The aging Earl, who frequented strip clubs in the French Quarter of New Orleans, falls in love with one of the burlesque stars, Blaze Starr.

When Earl and Blaze move in together, Earl's opponents use this to attack his controversial political program, which included civil rights for blacks in the 1950's. It was written and directed by Ron Shelton, and is based on the 1974 memoir *Blaze Starr: My Life as Told to Huey Perry* by Blaze Starr and Huey Perry.

The film starred Paul Newman as Earl Long and Lolita Davidovich as Blaze Starr. The real Blaze Starr (left) made a cameo appearance in the film.

Blaze was shot mostly on location in areas around Louisiana, including Asphodel Plantation. Other scenes were filmed in Long's hometown of Winnfield, Baton Rouge and New Orleans.

Dream Boy - 2008

See Greenwood Plantation.

BOCAGE PLANTATION
Darrow, Louisiana

Resting on some 100 acres on the east bank of the Mississippi River, Bocage Plantation is one of the jewels of the River Road plantations between New Orleans and Baton Rouge. The plantation house is a grand Greek Revival mansion.

Bocage Plantation was established in January 1801, five years after Étienne de Boré proved that sugarcane cultivation could be profitable in southern Louisiana and two years before the Louisiana Purchase.

The original mansion was a wedding gift from St. James Parish planter Marius Pons Bringier to his eldest daughter, 14-year-old Francoise "Fanny" Bringier (right) and her 34-year-old Paris born husband Christophe Colomb, on the occasion of their wedding. Colomb claimed to be a descendant of Christopher Columbus.

Fanny was born at White Hall Plantation in St. James Parish. Christophe was born in Corbille, France. The couple had eight children – Louis Arthur, Christophe Jr., Virginia, Amelina, Cedalie, Leapold, Pons, and Henry Octave. Local history states that Christophe was more interested in the finer things of life, music, painting, entertaining, etc., than working a plantation and that it was Fanny who took over the operations of Bocage. She handled everything from the management of the house to the cane fields.

Fanny passed away May 10, 1827 at Bocage Plantation, several years before Christophe died. Upon his death in 1832, their son Luis Arthur Colomb and his wife Mathilde de Lauzon Thibaut inherited Bocage.

For many years, the belief was that the original 1801 house was destroyed by fire and the current house was the result of a full remodeling of that building which took place around 1837. However, according to the National Park Service of the U.S. Department of Interior, a recent renovation of the home, which in some places involved the removal of exterior stucco and interior plaster, revealed no hint of the remodeling of an earlier building. During the process, the bases of four symmetrically placed chimneys surrounded by extensive charred remains and fragments of brick and broken glass were discovered buried about 40 feet behind the house. Experts involved in the recent renovation believe that these remains are of the original 1801 home and that the current building is a replacement for the one that burned.

Bocage was designed by an architect well skilled in the Greek Revival idiom. Although no documentary evidence exists to confirm the designer's identity, circumstantial evidence suggests that Luis Arthur and Mathilde were fortunate enough to have obtained the services of James Harrison Dakin, a New York architect for the design of their new home. Dakin relocated to Louisiana in 1835 and came under the Bringier family's employ. He would later design Louisiana's fine Gothic Revival Old State Capitol (1847-1849) in Baton Rouge.

Bocage's façade features square columns, an impressive entablature with a denticulated cornice, a pediment shaped parapet (which is unusual for Louisiana) and a double gallery.

Inside, the home has a Creole floor plan whose primary living space, called a premier etage, is located on the second floor. Interior rooms opening into each other without hallways and a rear cabinet-loggia range make up the plan. The grander rooms across the front open onto the upper gallery that overlooks the Mississippi River levee and provides a panoramic view of the 100-acre plantation. However, premier etage's most significant decorative feature is a splendid anthemion and patera door surround which encases a second-floor set of pocket doors. The design for this feature is taken directly from Plate 26 of Minard Lafever's 1835 builders' pattern book, *Beauties of Modern Architecture*, to which Dakin apparently contributed drawings.

In 1941, Bocage was purchased by Drs. E. G. Kohlsdorf and Anita Crozat Kohlsdorf (left). The new owners oversaw a massive renovation to repair the damage caused by having been vacant for several decades, while adding the necessary kitchen, bathrooms and electricity.

Dr. Marion Rundell, a native of Louisiana, purchased Bocage in 2008 and has returned the mansion to its original splendor."

The plantation was added to the National Register of Historic Places on June 20, 1991. Now an elegant bed and breakfast, the stately mansion is open for tours and group functions.

Bocage was featured in the 2013 film *12 Years a Slave*.

12 Years a Slave - 2013

12 Years a Slave is based on an incredible true story of one man's fight for survival and freedom. In the pre-Civil War United States, Solomon Northup, a free black man from upstate New York, is abducted and sold into slavery. Facing the cruelty of a malevolent slave owner, as well as unexpected kindnesses, Solomon struggles not only to stay alive, but to retain his dignity. In the twelfth year of his unforgettable odyssey, Solomon's chance meeting with a Canadian abolitionist forever alters his life.

The film stars Chiwetel Ejiofor, Michael Fassbender, Brad Pitt, Benedit Cumberbatch, Paul Giamatti, Lupita Nyong'o, and Alfre Woodard and was directed by Steve McQueen.

The photo above features director Steve McQueen and star Chiwetel Ejiofor discussing a scene.

The film shot at four Louisiana plantations, taking audiences into every sensory aspect of Louisiana plantations – the sights, sounds and smells, the relentless heat, the swarming insects, the wild, fetid swamps and the long, dark nights in slaves' quarters.

Bocage Plantation was used as the setting for the Shaw Farm. Felicity Plantation in Vacherie stood in for Epps' place. Standing in for Ford's pastoral place is the Magnolia Plantation in Schriever. The final plantation used in the film is Destrehan, as Epps' "gin house," where the cotton bales are counted. Other scenes were filmed in New Orleans.

12 Years a Slave is based on the book of the same name, which was written by the real Solomon Northup. While the film took some creative license, the characters and places featured in the film were real. The current Louisiana plantations used in the film stood in for real places. Below are images of the real Epps and Shaw Plantations, respectively, as they existed in the past.

BUENA VISTA PLANTATION
DeSoto Parish

Boykin Witherspoon, a South Carolina planter, began buying parcels of land for his plantation in 1839, and by the eve of the Civil War, had emerged as one of the wealthiest planters in the parish. He acquired about 360 acres of land from the federal government in De Soto Parish, Louisiana. Here he established Buena Vista Plantation and moved his family and slaves there.

The house is in a remote location well off the road, and the view is of the gently undulating countryside of rural DeSoto Parish. Buena Vista has received very few alterations and even retains its original kitchen dependency.

A building contract, which is very general in nature, reveals that Boykin Witherspoon contracted with M. Robbins on November 29, 1859 to build Buena Vista. Construction on the house began in 1859, five years after Witherspoon moved his family to Louisiana.

Buena Vista is a huge two-and-a-half story frame Greek Revival plantation house with a documented date of 1859. The name means "good view."

Buena Vista has a central hall plan with two rooms on each side. The front parlors are much larger than the two rooms in back. The floor plan upstairs is similar, except the rooms are of more equal size, and the builder shortened the central hall to allow for a front central bedroom.

The gallery has a full entablature and octagonal columns resting on brick piers the height of the gallery floor. The gallery floor begins about a foot behind the columns. The column capitals feature four bands of molding. The Gothic balustrade has balusters carved in a pointed arch shape with a sharp spike in the middle of each pattern.

The unusual multi-shaft newel posts are formed of pie shape sections that appear to be glued together. The towering aedicule style front doorway has a heavy cornice ornamented with dentils and a secondary tiny denticular cornice below the transom. The pilasters framing the door are fluted, while those defining the entire doorway have an inset molded panel with a delicate almost oriental-looking pointed arch top.

Like many locations in the south, the Buena Vista plantation was once used as a Civil War hospital.

The home is listed on the National Register.

Buena Vista was the location for the 1969 film *Slaves.*

Slaves - 1969

Slaves is a psychological drama of the relationships between whites and blacks set against a background of slavery as a social and economic institution. Stephen Boyd (below) portrays a former Boston slave ship captain who settles in the south and ruthlessly exploits the system of slavery. Dionne Warwick (below) , in her first motion picture, plays his mistress and Ossie Davis portrays a slave sold from near-freedom on a Kentucky horse farm to the harsh life on Boyd's cotton plantation. The film was directed by Herbert J. Biberman.

Slaves was filmed in its entirety on the 600 acre Buena Vista Plantation.

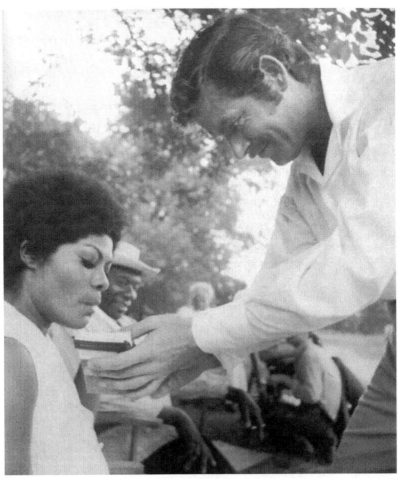

CALUMET PLANTATION
Patterson, Louisiana

The original land grant on which Calumet was built was to Jean Baptiste Bossier (right). It was initially known as the "O. and N. Cornay Plantation." The house was built in 1830 and was the home of Octave Cornay, who, with his brother, Numa, had built up a large sugar mill complex on land inherited from their mother, Mrs. Henry Cornay (nee Francoise Radeville Haydel), in an area known as Dutch Settlement. She had inherited from her parents, George Haydel and Marguerite Bossier.

Daniel Thompson and his wife Georgine "Geordy" Wibray Urquhart purchased the plantation in 1871, changing the name to Calumet. Thompson, who occupied it for thirty years until his death in 1900, was a sugar planter of great importance. He was a pioneer in the research and application of the chemical aspect of the sugar industry, and maintained a year-round study with laboratory analyses by chemists working in conjunction with the U. S. Department of Agriculture in Washington, D. C. His work was considered to be one of the most important contributions to the development and advancement of the sugar industry in the United States. His son, Wibray, continued his work for several years after his father's death.

Calumet is a 1-1/2 story center hall frame cottage with porches at the front and rear. The walls are composed of briquette entre poteaux. Federal style dormers and six-over-six windows provide a neoclassical character to the cottage style of the original house.

During the Civil War, Cornay/Calumet was the site of a number of engagements, most notably being the Battle of Bisland, in which 25,000 men were involved, and the naval encounters of the Confederate steamer "Cotton," which ended in flames at Cornay's bridge.

Patterson lumber magnate and aviation pioneer Harry Palmerson Williams owned Calumet during the early twentieth century. When Williams married film star Marguerite Clark in 1918, she was at the height of stardom, having moved from a career on the stage in New York to being the most highly paid movie actress in Hollywood.

Harry himself became famous as a pioneer in aviation, starting as a playboy pilot and ending up creating with his partner, Jimmy Wedell, the fastest racing planes in the world. At Calumet, opposite the home, was developed one of the first airports in the South and one of the first airplane manufacturing plants in the United States. Harry P. Williams & James R. Wendell, as Wendell-Williams Air Service, designed and built some of the fastest land-based airplanes of their time. Jimmie Wendell set many flying records, winning the Bendix & Thompson Trophies

Following two tragic plane crashes that caused the deaths of both Wendell and Williams, Marguerite Clark Williams sold her husband's U. S. Mail contracts and other contracts to Eastern Airlines, and donated the airport to the State of Louisiana. It is still in operation and has a fine museum dedicated to Wedell and Williams, containing some fascinating aeronautical memorabilia.

Clarence W. Baughman later operated Calumet as a sugar plantation until about 1956. Mr. and Mrs. William D. Hunter acquired the main house. Calumet Plantation, Inc. was formed on April 25, 1983.

Calumet Plantation was added to the National Register of Historic Places on October 18, 1983.

Calumet Plantation was featured in the 1959 film *Louisiana Hussy*. Other scenes filmed in Morgan City and Patterson and included the W. M. McKnight home at Idlewild Plantation.

Louisiana Hussy - 1959

Louisiana Hussy featured an alluring Cajun beauty who left disaster in her wake wherever she went. During the course of the film, the "hussy" destroyed several families, broke up quite a few marriages, and drove at least one unfortunate young girl to suicide. Nina finally got trapped in one of her own webs of sexual intrigue.

Nan Peterson, Peter Coe, Robert Richards and Betty Lynn starred in the film, which was directed by Lee Sholem.

Calumet Plantation serves as the home of Clay Lanier.

COTTAGE PLANTATION
East Baton Rouge Parish

The Cottage was built in 1824 by Colonel Abner Duncan as a wedding gift for his daughter Frances Sophia and her husband, Frederick Daniel Conrad. The Greek Revival mansion was set in a grove of live oaks.

Twelve Doric columns enclosed a brick-paved gallery and supported a wide second story gallery and dormered roof. The lower floor was brick, the upper was wood. The paneled doorway was flanked by fluted columns and sidelights and topped by a fan light. The house had 22 rooms and was considered one of the finest in the Baton Rouge area.

It soon became one of the most successful sugar plantations in the area. By the 1850's, the Conrads were entertaining many rich and powerful guests including such notables as Jefferson Davis, Henry Clay, Zachary Taylor, and the Marquis de Lafayette.

The Conrad family itself had esteemed beginnings, tracing its ancestry to George and Martha Washington. In the years before the Civil War, life was very good at the Cottage. They imported furniture, collected a fortune in jewelry and amassed great wealth.

In the 1850's, another man came to live at the Cottage - a traveling teacher named Angus Holt, who would become the private tutor to the Conrad children and Frederick Conrad's personal secretary. Holt became a part of the Conrad family and lived there happily until war came.

On the foggy Sunday morning of February 27, 1859, the four boilers of the *Princess*, a steam-powered riverboat, exploded near the Cottage, sending bodies and cargo flying in all directions. It was loaded with cotton and passengers bound for Mardi Gras in New Orleans. Conrad had his slaves help the victims to shore, and laid out bed sheets covered in flour on the lawn of the house on which to lay the wounded. The explosion left 70 dead, and many others wounded. The boat and its cargo were a total loss. Human error, failure to maintain safe boiler pressure, was determined to be the cause, and a pall was cast over the 1859 Mardi Gras celebrations.

Life, after the beginning of the Civil War, changed forever. The Union Army took over the Cottage and removed everything that could be found of value, from horses to furniture to jewelry to even the clothing of the children. The troops occupied the plantation and held the family prisoner, being especially brutal with Frederick Conrad and his secretary, Mr. Holt.

After the troops left, the family abandoned the house and it was taken over and used as a hospital for Union soldiers with yellow fever. In the years that followed, this is probably what saved it from being destroyed by vandals. Many had died from the disease in the house and were buried on the grounds. The fear that the sickness lingered kept many people away.

A few years later, Frederick Conrad died in New Orleans and Holt returned to the abandoned Cottage a changed man. He became a recluse, spending all of his time trying to repair the old house for what remained of the Conrad family, most of whom had been his students. He stopped shaving and was seen wandering the grounds of the Cottage with a long, white beard. Many local people avoided him, but they could never forget the wonderful man that he had once been. The neighbors made frequent gifts of food to sustain him while he stayed on at the house.

When Holt finally died, friends went through his many trunks and found huge quantities of books and clothing, along with moldy half-eaten biscuits and portions of meals. Holt had taken to walking about the house at night, reliving the happier times in the house. As he walked, he would munch on biscuits and meat and then throw the uneaten portion into one of his trunks. Holt was buried in a local cemetery.

As the years passed, the Cottage again stood empty. People who lived nearby said it was haunted. No one would go near the house after dark, fearing that Holt's ghost was still there. There were reports of doors opening and slamming by themselves and sightings of apparitions on the grounds. These shadowy figures were often seen, but when investigated, the place was found to be empty.

In 1917, the Cottage was used as the background for the silent film *Burning the Candle*. According to early film records, this was the first film shot on location in Baton Rouge and is one of the first examples of filmmakers using the plantations of Louisiana to give authenticity to their movies.

In the 1920's, the Conrad family began a restoration of the house. Luckily, thanks to the rumors of ghosts and yellow fever, the house had managed to survive fairly intact throughout the years. In the 1950's, the house was opened to the public and served as a museum to the memory of the Old South. It attracted a great deal of interest and artists came from all over the world to capture the flair of the south before the Civil War.

During this time, the rumors of ghosts still persisted. Some visitors would report the sounds of singing and strange music in the house and on the grounds. It seems that in the heyday of the house, before the war, the Conrads would often entertain their guests by having their slaves sing for them and play music. Now, nearly a century later, the sounds of that music could still be heard at the house, a residual and ghostly echo from another time.

Other visitors reported their own encounters with Mr. Holt. He was said to be seen walking through the house, pulling at his long beard and mumbling to himself. In 1940, one reporter for the *Elks Magazine* even photographed the ghost by accident. He was doing a story about the Cottage and after having his film developed, he noticed the image of an old man looking out the window. He was sure that no one had been there at the time and after showing it the staff members at the house identified the apparition as Mr. Holt!

On a February morning in 1960, the Cottage burned to the ground. The firemen who were on the scene would later report a very strange incident. It seemed that while they were directing water on the house from the side garden, a man appeared in the upper window of the house. The fire fighters directed him to jump, but he never seemed to notice them or the fire that was all around him. The roof suddenly collapsed and the man was gone. After the fire was put out, they sifted the debris, searching for the man's remains but found no body.

There are nothing but ruins (right) now where the Cottage once stood, but visitors to the property still claim to hear the sounds of music and singing there. They also claim to encounter the ghost of Mr. Holt as he wanders about the property.

In addition to **Burning the Candle**, 1917, two other films featured the Cottage,

Burning the Candle - 1917

American stage and film actors Henry B. Walthall and Mary Charleston came to Baton Rouge to film scenes for **Burning the Candle**. The film was directed by Harry Beaumont and released through Kleine-Edison-Selig-Essanay. The film projects a powerful lesson on the liquor theme.

The story involves a young southerner who goes to New York to accept a job soon after his married. Once in New York, the former non-drinker finds himself slowly becoming an alcoholic. He loses his job and his young wife returns to her southern home. After becoming a vagabond and losing family and friends, he decides to conquer his demons, regaining his position and his wife.

The Cottage served as the southern home featured in this film.

Cinerama Holiday - 1955

Cinerama Holiday was the second of the Cinerama films. Cinerama is a widescreen process that, originally, simultaneously projected images from three synchronized 35 mm projectors onto a huge, deeply curved screen. The trademarked process was marketed by the Cinerama Corporation. It was the first of a number of novel processes introduced during the 1950s, when the movie industry was reacting to competition from television. Cinerama was presented to the public as a theatrical event, with reserved seating and printed programs, and audience members often dressed in their best attire for the evening.

In this musical travelogue, two real life couples, John and Betty Marsh from Kansas City, and Fred and Beatrice Troller from Zurich, Switzerland, meet at the St. Louis Airport just before embarking on separate vacation adventures. The Marshes are en route to Europe, while the Trollers will simultaneously explore the United States. After several stops in the United States, the Trollers head to New Orleans where they attend a music-filled service at the Second Free Mission Baptist Church, visit the Lafayette Cemetery where they witness a funeral, and attend a music performance by the Original Dixieland Jazz Band at the Absinthe House nightclub. While touring the south, they visit the Cottage. *Cinerama Holiday* was directed by Robert Bendick.

Band of Angels - 1957

Based on the best seller written by Robert Penn Warren, the film is set in the south at the time of the Civil War. It focuses on the romance between Hamish Bond, a wealthy New Orleans gentleman and former slave runner, and a Southern plantation heiress, Amantha Starr. When her father dies, Amantha learns that her mother was a slave, making her property of the plantation. At a slave auction, she is purchased by Bond who makes her the mistress of his house. Clark Gable stars as Bond and Yvonne DeCarlo portrays Amantha.

The film, which also stars Sidney Poitier, Efrem Zimbalist, Jr. and Patric Knowles, was directed by Raoul Walsh.

The image below features DiCarlo, Gable and Walsh discussing a scene.

The filmmakers wanted to ensure an authentic feel to the film so it was shot on location at and around Baton Rouge.

The Cottage served as Pointe du Loup, the up-river plantation home of Bond where Amantha becomes house mistress. Ashland Belle Helene Plantation was also featured in the film as Belle Helene, another of Bond's plantation homes. It is from Belle Helene that Bond and Amanthe escape to the West Indies.

COTTAGE PLANTATION
West Feliciana Parish

The Cottage Plantation is located on U. S. Highway 61, six miles north of St. Francisville, Louisiana on the east side of the road. It sits on land secured by John Allen and Patrick Holland through a Spanish land grant in 1795.

The core home was built in 1795 and was about 42 feet in length. It was extended to 85 feet in the very early 1800's.   The two buildings form an "L" shape, with the original house as part of the foot of the L. The extension copied the architecture of the original building so that it appears to be one structure. The roof at the rear of the house was raised in the early 1800's to provide a gallery running the length of the house and it copied the front of the house. The last section of the house to be built was the great wing, or the side of the L, 65 feet long, whose front gallery adjoins the back gallery of the original building. A unique feature in its construction is that the whole length of the cornice is pierced by a series of louvers, serving the double purpose of ventilating and keeping the glare off the gallery. The architecture reflects both Spanish and English influence.   It was completed in 1859.

The Cottage is completely built of virgin cypress except for the massive sills which were made of various woods from the plantation.   The pillars on the galleries are hand wrought, as is the exterior and interior woodwork. There are twelve square rooms in the main house and four in the wing. The rooms in the main section of the house open onto the gallery through door-windows with stationary shutters. Every room is furnished with a handcarved fireplace mantle, some of extreme simplicity and others elaborate with fluted Doric columns and panels in a sunburst design.

Thomas Butler (right) acquired the Cottage Plantation around 1811. In 1813, he was appointed judge of the Louisiana Third District Court and later was elected to the U.S. Congress, serving as a representative from 1818 to 1821. Butler was a Louisiana gubernatorial candidate twice in the 1820's and lost both elections.

The Cottage was lived in by the Butler family until it was bought by J. E. Brown in 1951. The home was passed down to the heirs of Mr. and Mrs. J. E. Brown.

The TV movie *The Autobiography of Miss Jane Pittman* was filmed on location at The Cottage in 1974.

The Autobiography of Miss Jane Pittman - 1974

In the 1974 made-for-TV film *The Autobiography of Miss Jane Pittman*, Cecily Tyson (below) aged from 19 to 110 in the role of Jane Pittman, a fictional African-American woman whose life began in slavery and ended at the inception of the Civil Rights Movement.

When a northern journalist traveled to the racially polarized south of 1962 to interview Ms. Pittman for a potential book, her life unfolds in flashbacks. Based on the novel by Ernest J. Gaines, the film was directed by John Korty.

The slave quarters of the Cottage Plantation served as the home of Miss Pittman. Other scenes were filmed at the Ashland Belle Helene Plantation and areas around Baton Rouge.

DESTREHAN PLANTATION
St. Charles Parish

One of the oldest and best-documented buildings from the State's colonial period, Destrehan Plantation House represents three major phases of construction and illustrates the changes in architectural style in Louisiana.

Erected in 1787 by Charles Paquet, Destrehan Plantation was purchased by indigo planter Robert Antointe Robin De Logny and his family. De Logny contracted with Pacquet, a free mulatto carpenter, to build a raised house in the West Indies Creole style, and outbuildings to support his indigo plantation. Pacquet was given the use of six slaves to build the house. He was paid the grand sum of "one brute negro," a cow and a calf, 100 bushels of both corn and rice, and $100 in cash upon completion. This building contract, still on file at the parish courthouse in Hahnville, Louisiana, makes Destrehan Plantation the oldest documented house in the Lower Mississippi Valley.

Destrehan Plantation House consists of a central, two-story house with open galleries on three sides and flanking two-story wings separated from the main body of the house by the side galleries. The central unit, the oldest part of the house, is composed of masonry columns on the ground floor and wood columns on the upper. At one time a colonnade had surrounded the central unit. The roof is double- pitched all around.

Upon de Logny's death, Jean Noel Destrehan (left) purchased the property from his father-in-law's estate. During Jean Noel's lifetime, he was a cornerstone of Louisiana history. In 1803, Destrehan was appointed first Deputy Mayor of New Orleans, serving with brother-in-law Etienne deBore, who was appointed mayor. Jean Noel helped shape the economic situation of the South when he and deBore perfected the granulation of sugar.

Jean Noel was active in the political arena all his life and was well respected for his fairness and intelligence. Jean Noel became a driving force in the statehood process and the writing of the territorial and state law for the new state of Louisiana.

While under the ownership of the Destrehan family, both the house and grounds went through considerable periods of change. In the 19th century the major cash crop at Destrehan became sugarcane rather than indigo and the house went through two further phases of construction. The original gallery columns were replaced in the 1830s or 40s with massive Greek Revival Doric columns of plastered brick and the cornice was altered accordingly. Its original colonial appearance was altered with the post-colonial addition of semi-detached wings.

Ownership of Destrehan changed in 1825, when Stephen Henderson bought the plantation from the Destréhan estate. Henderson, a Scottish immigrant who arrived in the United States penniless, became an extremely wealthy entrepreneur. In 1815, at the age of 40, he married Marie Eléonore "Zelia" Destréhan, daughter of Jean-Noël Destréhan, who was 15 at the time of her marriage. Destrehan Plantation was Zelia's childhood home. Famed pirate Jean Lafitte was a personal friend of Henderson and visited Destrehan on multiple occasions. A childless Zelia died in 1830, and a grief-stricken Henderson followed eight years later.

Henderson's will was quite controversial as he instructed that all his slaves be freed, and for those that desired, be given transport to Liberia. For those that stayed, a factory was to be set up for the freed slaves to manufacture shoes and clothes, and 25 years after his death a city was to be laid out on the grounds of the plantation and named Dunblane. The family contested the will and after 12 years in litigation, and tried before the Louisiana Supreme Court, the will was set aside due to a technicality

Following Henderson's death, Pierre Adolphe Rost, (right) a justice on the Louisiana Supreme Court from 1845 to 1853, purchased the plantation from his estate in 1839. He and his wife, Louise Odile Destrehan, another daughter of Jean-Noël Destrehan, began to remodel the house in the then popular Greek Revival style. Doors and windows were trimmed in Greek Revival details, the columns were encased in plastered brick and the rear gallery was enclosed to make an entrance foyer. Also, removed from the corners of the rear gallery, winding staircases were re-installed in the center hall, and on the exterior, the stucco was scored to resemble stone.

On the advent of the American Civil War, Rost offered his services to the Confederate States of America and was assigned as the Confederate Representative to Spain, where he stayed with his family for most of the war.

In 1865, the plantation was seized by the Freedmen's Bureau and the Rost Home Colony was created. The colony was for the freedmen to have access to medical and educational aid, in addition to working for wages or for a portion of the crops. The Rost Home Colony was the most successful of those created in Louisiana and provided a profit to the Bureau.

In 1865, Pierre Rost returned home from Europe, with a pardon from President Andrew Johnson, and demanded his property back. The Colony existed for an additional year, paying Rost rent, and the last colonist left in December 1866. Pierre Rost died in 1868 and his wife and son, Emile Rost, continued to live at Destrehan Plantation. In 1910, Emile Rost sold the plantation to the Destrehan Planting and Manufacturing Company, ending family ownership of the estate after 123 years.

In 1914, the Mexican Petroleum Company, a predecessor of American Oil Company ("Amoco"), bought the property and built an oil refinery. The company tore down the ancillary buildings around the mansion and built employee housing. The mansion itself was used in a variety of ways including a clubhouse. In 1959, American Oil tore down the refinery, abandoning the site and the following twelve years brought rapid decay for Destrehan Plantation.

Thanks to an old legend that the illustrious privateer Jean Lafitte had hidden treasure in the house, treasure-seekers left gaping holes in the walls. Vandals also stripped the house of its Italian marble mantels, cypress paneling, Spanish tiles, and window panes. Fortunately, a local sheriff prevented the theft of the plantation's original 1840s iron gates and a 1,400 lb marble bathtub, rumored to be a gift from Napoleon Bonaparte to the family.

In 1968, a group of local friends, concerned for Destrehan Plantation's future, successfully petitioned Amoco Oil Company, owner of the property since the 1950s, to replace the old roof and to secure the property and house against intruders. The company also indicated a willingness to donate Destrehan to a non-profit group that would preserve the house.

In December 1971, the house and nearly four acres of land were deeded to the Society. At the same time, an adjacent tract nearly one hundred times that size was sold and ultimately developed as a business park. Destrehan Plantation is open seven days a week for guided tours which interpret the lives of the plantation's former residents—both free and enslaved.

Two major movies were filmed on location at Destrehan.

12 Years A Slave - 2013

See Bocage Plantation.

Interview with the Vampire - 1994

Interview with the Vampire was based on the bestselling novel written by New Orleans native Anne Rice. A vampire named Louis tells his 200-year-long life story to a reporter. In 1791, Louis is a young indigo plantation owner living south of New Orleans. Distraught by the death of his brother, he seeks death in any way possible. Louis is approached by a vampire named Lestat, who desires Louis' company. Lestat turns Louis into a vampire and the two become immortal companions. Lestat spends time feeding off the local plantation slaves while Louis, who finds it morally impossible for him to murder humans to survive, feeds from animals.

The film starred Tom Cruise (right), Brad Pitt, Antonio Bandera, Stephen Rea, Kirsten Dunst and Christian Slater. Director Neil Jordan (right) rewrote Rice's first draft of the screenplay, though she received sole credit.

Key scenes of *Interview with the Vampire* were at Destrehan Plantation (below). Oak Alley Plantation served as the Pointe du Lac family home. Other filming location included the original slave cabins at Laurel Valley Plantation and Home Place in Hahnville.

EVERGREEN PLANTATION
Edgard, Louisiana

Evergreen Plantation is the most intact plantation complex in the south with 37 buildings on the National Register of Historic Places, including 22 slave cabins. Evergreen has the country's highest historic designation and joins Mount Vernon and Gettysburg in being granted landmark status for its agricultural acreage.

The story of Evergreen begins with the arrival of the Germans at the port of New Orleans in the 1700s. Ambroise Heidel (which became Haydel) and his five sons lived along the west bank of the Mississippi. The extended family eventually owned five miles of river frontage on the so-called German Coast. Ambroise's son Christophe, considered a Creole by virtue of intermarriage with a local French family, built the big house in 1790 as a Louisiana Colonial, or Creole farmhouse. Indigo was the predominant crop in the 1700's. Slaves did the field work and may have built the house for Christophe and his wife, Charlotte Oubre. Christophe's brother built Whitney Plantation next door.

Christophe's daughter, Magdelaine Heidel Becnel, inherited the plantation when he and his wife died in 1799. There, Magdelaine raised her eight children and her young, orphaned grandson, Pierre Clidamant Becnel, whose parents died of yellow fever. In that day, it was customary to marry your cousins, and four of Magdelaine's children married four Heidel first cousins who lived next door at Whitney. Magdelaine died in 1830 at the age of 75. Pierre Clidamant Becnel bought out the other heirs to his grandmother's home. He had a great interest in architecture and traveled to Philadelphia for a year to study Greek Revival design.

In 1832, he reconstructed the ancestral family home, giving it a stunning Greek Revival exterior while retaining the French Creole interior floor plan. As a result of this expansion, the "big house" features stuccoed-brick Doric columns that extend from the ground to the roof on the wide double galleries, and boasts two remarkable fanlight doorways at the head and foot of the winding double stairway servicing the galleries.

The contract with the builder, John Carter from St. Charles Parish, still exists. It called for enclosing the open basement and adding three rooms, raising the existing floor two feet and raising the roof 31 inches. There was to be the appearance of a terrace or balcony on the roof, and "two winding stairs of grace and elegance." The contract also noted that Carter and his two assistants would receive "bed, board and washing during execution of the work." Carter's pay was $1,800 at the start of the job and the same amount at completion.

Pierre was quite the recycler. He stipulated in the contract, "Do the work in such a way as to prevent a useless waste of materials." Approximately 300,000 bricks from Uncle Sam Plantation (dismantled because the levee was being moved) were ferried across the river for use in the reconstruction. In redesigning the family home, Pierre fell into bankruptcy in 1835 and was forced to sell to his cousin, Lezin Becnel, who graciously allowed Pierre and his wife, Desiree Brou, to continue to live in the house. Evergreen was owned by the Becnels until it was sold in 1894 to Alfred and Edward Songy. For 100 years, the place had been called The Becnel Plantation, but the Songys named it Evergreen.

The Songy family resided at Evergreen until 1930 when, after a trifecta of misfortunes—a 1927 flood, mosaic disease of the sugar cane, and financial strains from the Great Depression—the bank foreclosed on the property. The Songys were forced to depart, leaving Evergreen unoccupied for 14 years, except for the cypress cabins, where farming families lived. Meanwhile, the big house and its dependencies were used to stable cattle and farm animals.

After being neglected and forlorn for about 14 years, philanthropist and oil heiress Matilda Geddings Gray (right) of Lake Charles acquired the property in 1946. To help her re-do her country estate, she turned to New Orleans architect Richard Koch, who was known for his restoration of historic Natchez properties and Oak Alley. Gray was one of several preservationists rescuing plantation homes from death by decay around that time. Others were the Crozats at Houmas House, the Stewarts at Oak Alley and the Judices at L'Hermitage, all on River Road.

Matilda Geddings Gray died in 1971. She had no children, no nephews and only one niece—Matilda Gray Stream, her brother's daughter, who was named after her. For more than 40 years, Matilda Stream's life has focused on the world that her aunt left her. Evergreen remained a private home for 60 years until Stream opened it for tours in 1998.

Evergreen is significant not only because of the existence of its main building along River Road, but also because of the remains of the plantation complex. With two pigeonniers (structures used by upper-class French for housing pigeons), two garconieries (dwellings for a family's young boys), a privy, a kitchen, a guesthouse, an overseer's house, and a double row of 22 slave cabins, Evergreen is unique. It is one of only a handful of plantations that evoke what major plantations resembled in the antebellum period of America's history.

The movie industry has featured Evergreen in the following films.

Abe Lincoln Vampire Hunter - 2012

Visionary filmmakers Tim Burton and Timur Bekmambetov reinvent the time-honored genre and present the terrifying creatures of the night as they were meant to be experienced -- as fierce, visceral, intense and bloodthirsty. *Abraham Lincoln Vampire Hunter* brings to the screen the secret life of our nation's favorite president . . . as history's greatest hunter of the undead. It is based on best-selling novel *Abraham Lincoln, Vampire Hunter*.

The film stars Benjamin Walker (below), Dominic Cooper, Anthony Mackie, Mary Elizabeth Winstead, Rufus Sewell, Marton Csokas. It was directed by Russian born filmmaker Timur Bekmambetov (below).

To achieve a natural feel to the time period, the film was shot almost entirely on location at Evergreen Plantation, where the mansion served as the White House.

Django Unchained - 2012

Set in the South two years before the Civil War, **Django Unchained** stars Jamie Foxx as Django, a slave whose brutal history with his former owners lands him face-to-face with German-born bounty hunter Dr. King Schultz (Christoph Waltz). Schultz is on the trail of the murderous Brittle brothers, and only Django can lead him to his bounty. The unorthodox Schultz acquires Django with a promise to free him upon the capture of the Brittles – dead or alive. Success leads Schultz to free Django, though the two men choose not to go their separate ways. Instead, Schultz seeks out the South's most wanted criminals with Django by his side. Honing vital hunting skills, Django remains focused on one goal: finding and rescuing Broomhilda (Kerry Washington), the wife he lost to the slave trade long ago.

Django and Schultz's search ultimately leads them to Calvin Candie (Leonardo DiCaprio), the proprietor of "Candyland," an infamous plantation. Exploring the compound under false pretenses, Django and Schultz arouse the suspicion of Stephen (Samuel L. Jackson), Candie's trusted house slave. Their moves are marked, and a treacherous organization closes in on them. If Django and Schultz are to escape with Broomhilda, they must choose between independence and solidarity, between sacrifice and survival. The film was written and directed by Quentin Tarantino,

The southern scenes for Django Unchained were filmed on location at Evergreen Plantation (below). The home doubled as Bennett Manor. Exterior scenes included the slave quarters and the sugar cane fields, which doubled as the grounds for Candyland.

FELICITY PLANTATION
St. James Parish

Felicity Plantation was built in 1846 by Francois Gabriel Valcour Aime (below) as a wedding gift to his daughter. Valcour Aime, born in St. Charles Parish in 1797, was well-connected in New Orleans and in the St. James Parish plantation country along the Mississippi River. In 1819, he married Josephine Roman, sister of Gov. André Bienvenu Roman, also a sugar planter. A.B. Roman led Louisiana from 1831 to 1835 and again from 1839 to 1844. Aime was so wealthy that he was sometimes called the Louis XIV of Louisiana.

Besides trading in real estate and raising sugar cane, he was an amateur scientist who experimented with techniques for refining sugar. He is credited with perfecting the vacuum pan method and was one of the only planters who refined sugar directly from cane juice on site. His innovative technique gave him a competitive edge and made him the richest man in Louisiana, with an estate valued in the millions.

Aime's fortune was at its zenith when his second daughter, Emma Félicité (below) married Septime Fortier. The planter gave Felicity Plantation to them as a wedding gift, and the Fortiers had 14 children there (although not all lived through childhood.)

The antebellum home has elements of French Colonial and Anglo-American styles and is built of cypress with six square wooden columns. It has wide central hallways on both the upper and lower floors. Several of the rooms contain red Italian marble mantelpieces. The 2-1/2 story home has attic dormers and galleries at ground and second levels in the front and rear.

In the early 1850s, they hired Frenchman Elisée Reclus as a live-in tutor. Reclus is described as "the foremost geographer of his epoch and a major figure in the history of anarchist political theory."

The tutor chronicled his years at Felicity in a memoir called "Fragment d'un voyage à la Nouvelle Orléans." Scholars of his work believe his years with the Aime-Fortier family were important in the development of his theories as it exposed him to "the cruel inhumanity of slavery." He reportedly left Louisiana because of it, writing that he "could not continue to earn money by tutoring the children of slave holders and thus steal from the Negroes who have truly earned through their sweat and blood the money that I put in my pocket."

In 1854, Félicité's brother Gabriel died of yellow fever at Le Petit Versailles, Aime's plantation. The death of his only son crushed the spirit of Valcour Aime, who wrote in his diary, "Let him who wishes continue. My time is finished." Aime suffered more heartbreak when his wife died in 1856 and his youngest daughter died in 1858. It is reported that Aime, in despair, moved into a small cottage on the grounds, spending much of his time praying in a chapel there.

Though his fortunes were declining, he donated valuable assets to the Marist fathers in 1861, enabling them to re-open Jefferson College (now Manresa in Convent), which had burned and closed 20 years before. When Aime died in 1867, his business and property were in disarray. The property was soon sold to pay debts. Le Petit Versailles burned in 1920, and today the only vestige of Aime's estate is a historical marker at the side of the road.

Several films were shot on location at Felicity.

Skeleton Key - 2005

The Skeleton Key centers around Caroline, a young hospice nurse, who is hired to tend to the very old and dying Ben Devereaux.

Devereaux lives in a huge Terrebonne Parish Louisiana mansion, where he's watched over by his wife, Violet. Caroline soon discovers that a pair of century-old spirits haunts the mansion. The spirits are evil and are manipulating the living to fit their desires.

Caroline herself is at the center of one of their sinister schemes and becomes entangled in a supernatural mystery involving the house, its former inhabitants, and the hoodoo rituals and spells that took place there. Intrigued by the mysterious home, Caroline begins to explore the old mansion. Armed with a skeleton key that unlocks every door, she discovers a hidden attic room that holds a deadly and terrifying secret.

The film starred Kate Hudson (below), Gena Rowlands (below), Peter Sarsgaard, John Hurt (below), and Joy Bryant.

The Skeleton Key was directed by Iain Softley (below).

All the King's Men - 2006

Scenes include the inside parlor and the driveway in front. See Albania Plantation.

12 Years a Slave - 2012

Felicity Plantation stood in for the home of Edwin Epps. See Bocage Plantation.

GOODWOOD PLANTATION
Baton Rouge, Louisiana

In 1776, King George III of England granted Thomas Hutchings 2,000 acres of land, which would eventually be known as Goodwood Plantation. Parts of this land are shown to be some of the most elevated sections in Baton Rouge with levels as high as 52 feet. The plantation was the center of a thriving sugar cane industry. During the 19th century, the plantation had thoroughbred horse racing with a one-mile racetrack. Approximately 25 years after receiving the grant, Mr. Hutchings died.

Dr. Samuel G. Laycock and his family moved to Baton Rouge from Ohio. Between the years of 1852-1856, Dr. Laycock built a house that was a replica of the "Goodwood House," home of the Duke Of Richmond, in West Sussex, England. The 15 room structure reflects the influence of English Georgian architecture, relatively uncommon in Louisiana.

The home is constructed of brick covered with cement with an English approach to Greek Revival Style--characterized by a restrained decorative program and rigid geometric symmetry. It has broad, iron-railed galleries supported by four Doric columns across the front.

According to a number of sources, Goodwood Plantation was the first house in Baton Rouge to have running water. Each room featured built-in washstands with marble tops and hand-painted Wedgwood China washbowls, which were serviced by water brought by wooden pipes from large attic cisterns.

The plantation was later owned by Charles Lewis Matthews and his wife, Penelope Stewart. In the early 1930's, Louis Winbourne Babin and his wife, Belle Stanard Babin, purchased the plantation. Mr. Babin, along with Cyrus J. Brown (aka C.J. Brown) and John T. Laycock, joined together in 1932 to develop 350 acres of the plantation known as "Goodwood Place." Members of the Babin family continue to reside in the home, which is the centerpiece of a Baton Rouge neighborhood known as "Old Goodwood."

Scenes from the 1967 film *Hurry Sundown*, directed by Otto Preminger, were shot at Goodwood.

Hurry Sundown - **1967**

Otto Preminger directed this star-studded adaptation of K.B. Gliden's novel about racial prejudice and emotional unrest in the Deep South. The film takes place in a small Georgia farm town in the months following World War II. A ruthless speculator attempts to complete a deal to sell his wife's land to a real estate developer. However, two parcels of land have escaped his reach, and he is determined to get them. One of the parcels is owned by a white veteran who has just returned home. The other is owned by the mother of a black veteran. The two families join forces against the landowner, which leads to violent reprisals against them.

The film starred Michael Caine, Jane Fonda, John Phillip Law, Diahann Carroll, Robert Hooks, Faye Dunaway, Burgess Meredith, Robert Reed, George Kennedy, Frank Converse and Loring Smith. It was produced and directed by Otto Preminger.

Although the film is set in Georgia, it was actually filmed entirely on location in Louisiana, particular the Goodwood Plantation in Baton Rouge (below) . It was the first major motion picture to star black actors to ever be shot on location in the south. The cast and crew received death threats from the Ku Klux Klan, had their car tires slashed, and had to be protected by armed state troopers.

GREENWOOD PLANTATION
West Feliciana Parish

Planter William Ruffin Barrow came from the North Carolina to West Feliciana Parish shortly after 1803. Selecting a tract of 12,000 acres in the most beautiful section of the Feliciana country, he began building brick kilns, cutting lumber and getting ready for the mansion he planned to build.

Greenwood Plantation, one of the Barrow dynasty of homes in West Feliciana Parish, was originally built in 1830. In the 1830's, Greenwood operated as a 3000 acre cotton plantation. In 1850, Barrow switched to sugar cane. Greenwood grew to 12,000 acres with 750 slaves.

The Greek Revival mansion took approximately four years to build, using quantities of costly wood-work and other materials which were brought from the North for the interior finish. It has twenty-eight massive columns with wide surrounding porches. A wide hall reaches from the front to the rear of the home. In the rear, a mahogany stairway winds to the floor above. At its peak, the plantation boasted forty extra buildings, including a coach house, stable, kitchen and smoke house. A slave village laid to the right featured a hundred brick cabins, a church, a hospital, a place for amusements, bath, etc., everything needed for a fully-functioning colony.

Fearing the loss of his fortune with the impending Civil War, Barrow sold Greenwood to John Stevenson who bought the home as a wedding present for his daughter Arabella "Bella" and her husband Charles Henry Reed. The Reeds were able to hold on to Greenwood Plantation until the latter part of the war. Union troops looted the property and destroyed nearly all of the plantation's some 100 ancillary structures. They spared the mansion which the Union used as a hospital.

Mr. and Mrs. Frank Percy purchased the neglected property in 1915 and restored the house, opening it to the public in 1940. On August 1, 1960, fire from a lightning strike completely destroyed all but the columns. The fact that the house was stucco over wood frame made it vulnerable; the columns, however, were stuccoed brick.

In 1968, Walton Barnes purchased the plantation home and 300 acres. He and his son, Richard, set out to rebuild the home. They wanted to restore Greenwood to its former glory. After spending many years researching and locating photographs of the home, the home was mostly finished by November, 1984.

At this time, a French-Canadian filmmaker contracted to use Greenwood for the movie *Louisiana*. During the filming of this movie, the filmmaker completed the landscaping and decorating of the home.

Besides *Louisiana*, Greenwood Plantation has also been featured in a number of films.

Drango - 1957

Set in a fictional burned-out Georgia town in the months immediately following the American Civil War, the film depicts the efforts of a resolute Union Army officer, Major Clint Drango (right) to set up a military governorship.

The townspeople are bitter over the destruction of their homes and are unaware that Drango had participated in the destruction of the town during Sherman's March.

Along with his aide Captain Banning, Drango is determined to heal the land he had previously harmed. Renegade former Confederates under Clay Allen plan to undermine Drango's benign administration in hopes of restarting the war.

The film starred Jeff Chandler, Joanne Dru, Julie London, Donald Crisp, Ronald Howard and John Lupton. It was produced by Jeff Chandler's own production company Earlmar Productions, and was written and directed by Hall Bartlett.

Exterior shots of **Drango** were shot on location at Greenwood Plantation (see below).

Louisiana - 1984

This three-part HBO miniseries focused on the life and travails of a 19th century southern belle named Virginia Tregan, her ruthless devotion to her husband's Louisiana cotton plantation called Bagatelle, and her love for the plantation's overseer.

When Virginia returned to her Louisiana home in 1836 after years of school in Paris, she finds that the plantation and its holdings have been sold to pay off family debts. Determined to recoup her personal fortune, she manipulates the breakup of an affair between her wealthy godfather and his mistress in order to marry him and become the mistress of Bagatelle. The film starred Margot Kidder, Ian Charleson, Andréa Ferréol, Len Cariou, Lloyd Bochner, Victor Lanoux, and Hilly Hicks and was directed by Philippe deBroca.

Greenwood filled in as Virginia's beloved plantation Bagatelle.

North and South, Books 1 and 2 - 1985, 1986

North and South Book 1 and *North and South Book 2* are two miniseries broadcast on ABC television in 1985 and 1986, respectively. Each miniseries was comprised of six episodes.

The story is set before, during, and immediately after the American Civil War. Based on the 1980s novels *North and South* by John Jakes, the film tells the story of the enduring friendship between Orry Main of South Carolina and George Hazard of Pennsylvania, who become best friends while attending the United States Military Academy at West Point. They later find themselves and their families on opposite sides of the war.

The slave-owning Mains are rural planters, while the Hazards, who resided in a small Northern mill town, live by manufacturing and industry. Their differences reflected the divisions between North and South that eventually led to the Civil War

The miniseries starred Patrick Swayze, James Read, Kirstie Alley, Georg Stanford Brown, David Carradine, Philip Casnoff, and Lesley-Anne Down (cast photo above). Book I was directed by Richard T. Heffron and Book II was directed by Kevin Connor.

Greenwood Plantation served as Resolute, the plantation home owned by the film's character Justin LaMotte.

Sister Sister - 1987

See Madewood Plantation.

Stormswept - 1995

On a storm swept summer night, a group of filmmakers find themselves trapped inside a haunted Louisiana mansion where a gorgeous young woman is secretly living. The six people become tormented by the spirit of a 200-year-old slave master with an insatiable erotic appetite who causes the women in the group to take their clothes off.

Directed by David Marsh, the film starred Justin Carroll, Kathleen Kinmont, Melissa Anne Moore.

Greenwood was featured as the Louisiana mansion at the heart of this film (below).

Dream Boy - 2008

A shy Louisiana teenager and his family move from Lake Charles to St. Francisville to escape the domestic disintegration within their own home. The family lives a quiet life on a farm. When a new boy moves in next door, the boys strike up a friendship as high school study partners. Their strong emotional bond soon takes a turn toward physical passion, a secret they must hide from those around them in the backwoods rural community. It was adapted from Jim Grimsley's novel.

The film starred Stephan Bender, Max Roeg, Thomas Jay Ryan, Diana Scarwid, Randy Wayne, Owen Beckman, Tom Gilroy, Tricia Mara, Rickie Lee Jones, Nick Ericson. It was directed by James Bolton.

Dream Boy was filmed on location at the Greenwood Plantation, Asphodel Plantation, as well as locations around St. Francisville and Baton Rouge.

Loss of a Teardrop Diamond - 2010

Some scenes filmed at Greenwood. See St. Louis Plantation.

The Host - 2013

The Host is based on the bestselling novel by author Stephenie Meyer. The story involves a group of small parasitic aliens that are taking over humans.

The "Souls," as they are known, travel to distant planets en masse, inserting themselves into a host body of that planet's dominant species, completely replacing the host's consciousness, although they are able to access their memory. The films heroine Melanie Stryder risks everything to protect those she cares most about.

The film stars Saoirse Ronan, Max Irons, Jake Abel, Chandler Canterbury and William Hurt. It was directed by Andrew Niccol.

The film was partially shot on location in Louisiana, including scenes featuring Greenwood Plantation (above)

Bonnie and Clyde - 2013

Bonnie and Clyde is a 2013 miniseries about Great Depression-era outlaws Bonnie and Clyde. The two-part TV movie is based on the true story of Clyde Barrow and Bonnie Parker. Barrow, a charismatic convicted armed robber, sweeps Parker – a young and impressionable, petite, small-town waitress, who is already married – off her feet. In the early 1930s, the two embark on one of the most infamous crime sprees in American history.

The miniseries stars Emile Hirsch (below), Holliday Grainger (below), William Hurt, Holly Hunter, Lane Garrison and Sarah Hyland and was directed by Bruce Beresford.

Bonnie and Clyde was filmed extensively around Louisiana including Baton Rouge, Donaldsonville, St. Francisville and Greenwood Plantation.

G. I. Joe Retaliation - 2013

This sequel to *G.I. Joe: The Rise of Cobra* begins with the G.I. Joe team being framed for crimes against the country by Zartan, disguised as the President. The Cobra Commander has all the world leaders under his influence, with their advanced warheads headed towards innocent populaces around the world. Outnumbered and outgunned, the surviving team members form a plan with their original leader, General Joseph Colton, to rescue the President and face off Cobra Commander, his accomplices and the world leaders.

G. I. Joe Retaliation was directed by Jon M. Chu and starred Dwayne Johnson, Jonathan Pryce Channing Tatum, Ray Park, Luke Bracey.

Almost the entire movie, aside from some mountain shots photographed in British Columbia, was filmed in Louisiana. Greenwood Plantation stood in for the U.S. President's vacation home (below).

Bad Country - 2014

The film opens with the following title card: "In the spring of 1983 a single arrest led a cop to an informant in southern Louisiana. Together they brought down a criminal empire."

When Baton Rouge police detective Bud Carter busts contract killer Jesse Weiland, he convinces Jesse to become an informant and rat out the South's most powerful crime ring. So when the syndicate orders Carter's death and Weiland's ID'd as a snitch, the two team up to take down the mob and the crime boss who ordered the hit. The film was inspired by true events that unfolded in the Capital City 30 years ago.

Film director Chris Brinker died suddenly in February at the age of 42 while the movie, previously titled Whiskey Bay, was in post-production. Tom Berenger, Neal McDonough, and Christopher Denham starred.

While the majority of the film was shot at Angola Prison, some scenes were filmed at Greenwood Plantation

HOME PLACE PLANTATION
St. Charles Parish

Home Place Plantation, designated a National Historic Landmark in 1970, is located on the west bank of the Mississippi River in St. Charles Parish. Between the years 1785 and 1791, Pierre Gaillard, or his widow, built Home Place Plantation on a Spanish land grant of 10,000 acres. It was possibly constructed by Charles Paquet, the same free man of color who built Destrehan Plantation, just across the river.

Home Place is a near perfect example of a raised Creole plantation house. It is one of the finest and least altered examples of a large French Colonial raised cottage left standing. Similar in plan to another National Historic Landmark, Parlange in Point Coupee Parish, Home Place is two rooms deep and four rooms across with a 16 foot-wide gallery on all sides, providing separate access to each of the second story rooms for cross ventilation. The upper story walls are constructed of cypress timbers in-filled with clay and Spanish moss. The lower story, with its thick brick walls and floors, contained seven service rooms, including the large dining room, a pantry, two wine rooms, a hall, and two storage rooms. The wine rooms still retain some of the original wine racks and the dining room walls are decorated in original green-gray and white Italian marble tiles

Once the center of a large sugar plantation, Home Place was originally surrounded by slave's quarters, pigeonniers (structures used by upper-class French for housing pigeons), a carriage house, and other dependencies used in plantation operations. Only the carriage house remains to the right rear of the house. Interesting features of the house include brick pillars at the south end that once supported a large wooden cistern that supplied water to the house.

In 1806 the widow Gaillard sold the home and property to Louis Edmond Fortier, and over the next twenty years of his ownership, he added considerable land to his holdings. Among the interests of Mr. Fortier was the raising of thoroughbred horses.

Edmond Fortier died in 1849, and his wife sold the home to their son Drausin and three of their sons-in-law. Drausin died of yellow fever in 1856. After Drausin's death of yellow fever in 1856, it became the property of Braddish Johnson in 1883.

In 1889, it was purchased by Pierre Anatole Keller and his brother-in-law, Ulysses Haydel. They divided it, with Keller retaining the upriver portion, with the home. Haydel held ownership of the downriver portion. Stairs were added to the front of the house in 1900. In 1904, Keller and his son Theodore began renovating the old home, which was by now called Keller-Homeplace. In addition to major alterations, they planted an allee of pecan trees up the front drive. According to National Park Service, The Keller family continues to own the property today.

Home Place Plantation was featured in the following films.

Convicts - **1991**

Set upon a struggling turn-of-the-century Texas sugar-cane plantation, a 13-year-old boy goes to work on the farm to earn enough money to buy a headstone for his father's grave. The plantation is run by senile Civil War veteran Soll Gautier, whose ill health and obsession with the convict labor he uses to work the farm, make it unlikely that the boy will ever be paid. The story is adapted from Horton Foote's cycle of plays The *Orphan's Home*. The film, directed by Peter Masterson, starred Robert Duvall, Lukas Haas, James Earl Jones and Horace Robedaux.

Home Place Plantation served as Soll Gautier's home (below).

Interview with the Vampire - **1994**

See Destrehan Plantation.

HOUMAS HOUSE
Ascension House

The first owners of the plantation were the indigenous Houmas Indians, who were given a land grant to occupy the fertile plain between the Mississippi and Lake Maurepas to the north.

The Houmas sold the land to Maurice Conway and Alexander Latil in the mid 1700's. The original French Provincial house that Latil erected on the property was a more modest home that reflected both the French and Spanish architectural influences that still define Louisiana's heritage. The smaller residence that also houses the kitchen was the original Latil House. It is situated directly behind the mansion, adjoined by a carriageway to the grand home described during its antebellum heyday as "The Sugar Palace." The original home was later used as living quarters for the staff that served the great house. By the time of the Louisiana Purchase in 1803, the plantation was established and producing sugar.

In 1810, Revolutionary War hero Gen. Wade Hampton of Virginia purchased the property and shortly thereafter began construction on the mansion. However, it was not until 1825 when Hampton's daughter, Caroline, and her husband, Col. John Preston, took over the property that the grand house truly began to take shape. As was often the practice in those days, the great house grew in stages and reached its final full dimension in 1840.

The Mansion is an excellent example of the peripteral type of Greek Revival architecture in which the main structure is surrounded by grand columns, each with an uninterrupted span from ground level to the roofline. Among Houmas House Plantation and Gardens' unique features are twin Garconierre, very rare among plantation homes. Federal arched dormers stand above the large Doric galleries.

Irishman John Burnside bought the plantation in 1857 for $1 million. A businessman and a character, Burnside increased production of sugar until Houmas House was the largest producer in the country, actively working the crop on 98,000 acres. During the Civil War, Burnside saved the mansion from destruction at the hands of advancing Union forces by declaring immunity as a subject of the British Crown. In addition to building a railway to carry his products to market —"The Sugar Cane Train (1862)" — Burnside, a bachelor, is also said to have offered payment to any parents in the parish who would name their sons "John."

An avid sportsman who wagered heavily in horse races, Burnside once secretly purchased a champion thoroughbred back East with the intent of defeating the steeds of fellow local businessmen in a big race. He quietly slipped the racehorse into the billiard room of the mansion where it was "stabled" until Burnside's surprise was unveiled at the starting line and hailed in the winner's circle.

Houmas House flourished under Burnside's ownership, but it was under a successor, Col. William Porcher Miles (right), that the plantation grew to its apex in the late 1800's when it was producing a monumental 20 million pounds of sugar each year. In 1927, the Mississippi came out of its banks in the epic "great flood." While Houmas House was spared, the surrounding areas were inundated. The ensuing economic havoc was but a prelude to the devastation of the Great Depression just two years later. Houmas House Plantation withered away. The mansion closed and fell into disrepair, a condition in which it remained until 1940 when Dr. George B. Crozat purchased it.

Crozat bought Houmas House to be a summer home away from his native New Orleans. He renovated the property with the intent to give it a more "Federal" look than the stately Greek Revival style in which it was conceived. The structure was painted white inside and out. Crown moldings and ceiling medallions were removed and both interior and exterior forms and finishes were simplified.

Eventually, the Crozat heirs opened the property to tourists. In 1963, the defining Bette Davis film *Hush, Hush Sweet Charlotte* was shot in the property. The room in which Ms. Davis stayed while filming is preserved as part of today's Houmas House tour.

When New Orleans businessman and preservationist Kevin Kelly fulfilled a lifelong dream by purchasing the home in early summer, 2003, he set about recreating the experience of encountering Houmas House circa 1840.

In addition to *Hush, Hush Sweet Charlotte*, other films shot on location include the following.

Hush, Hush Sweet Charlotte - 1963

Following the unexpected 1962 box-office hit *What Ever Happened to Baby Jane?*, director Robert Aldrich wanted to re-team stars Joan Crawford and Bette Davis. He found the perfect property in **Hush Hush Sweet Charlotte**, based on the short story *Hush Now...Sweet Charlotte* by Henry Farrell, the author of *What Ever Happened to Baby Jane?*.

When the Louisiana Highway Commission decides to build a road through her property, Charlotte Hollis threatens the workmen with a shotgun. Thirty-seven years earlier Charlotte's married lover, John Mayhew, was murdered; and though the killer was never discovered, the local townspeople are convinced of Charlotte's guilt. Charlotte herself, believing that her father killed Mayhew, became a recluse, living with her housekeeper, Velma, in the deteriorating Hollis mansion. She sought help in her fight against the Highway Commission from Miriam, a poor cousin who lived with the family as a girl. The cousin, however, had sinister plans of her own.

The film starred Bette Davis, Olivia de Haviland (who replaced an ill Joan Crawford during shooting), Joseph Cotton, Agnes Moorehead, Cecil Kellaway, Victor Buono, Mary Astor and Wesley Addy.

The cast and crew arrived in Louisiana in the early summer of 1964 to shot location footage for the film. Scenes were shot at the Houmas House and Oak Alley Plantation (above).

Moon of the Wolf - 1972

Moon of the Wolf was a made-for-television Gothic horror film first broadcast on September 26, 1972, on ABC Movie of the Week.

After several townspeople are savagely murdered, a sheriff in the Louisiana bayous searches for a crazed killer. After analyzing a series of bizarre clues, he becomes convinced that he's chasing a modern-day werewolf.

It starred David Janssen (right), Barbara Rush, Geoffrey Lewis and Bradford Dillman, with a script by Alvin Sapinsley (based on Leslie H. Whitten's novel of the same name).

The film was directed by Daniel Petrie and filmed on location at Houmas House. All of the downtown footage was shot in Clinton, Louisiana.

Mandingo - 1975

See Ashland Belle Plantation.

Big Bob Johnson and his Fantastic Speed Circus - 1978

Big Bob is the leader of three daredevil race car drivers. He makes a brief pit stop to save a deserving young man from being swindled out of his inheritance by his devious uncle Their efforts resulted in a race from one end of Louisiana to the other that pitted one Rolls-Royce against another.

This made-for-TV movie (and unsuccessful TV pilot) starred Charles Napier, Maud Adams, Constance Forslund, Rick Hurst, William Daniels and Burton Gilliam. It was directed by Jack Starrett.

The film was shot on location at Houmas House and around Baton Rouge

A Woman Called Moses - 1979

See Madewood Plantation.

Fletch Lives - 1988

See Ashland Belle Helene Plantation.

Snow Wonder - 2005

This made-for-TV movie aired on CBS Network November 20, 2005. As a magical Christmas snowstorm blows across the country, small miracles change the lives of various people.

Paula, a maid-of-honor at her best friend's wedding, realizes that her unrequited love for the groom isn't so unrequited.

Bev, a recently widowed woman, flees to New Mexico to escape memories of her husband's favorite holiday.

Pilar, a divorced mother, dreads the idea of her son spending Christmas with his abusive father.

Luke is stranded in his tiny apartment with his crazy Aunt Lula and is amazed when she reveals the secret romances she had with some famous actor.

Marjean discovers the truth about her philandering husband.

The cast included Julie Ann Emery, Jennifer Esposito, Camryn Manheim, Poppy Montgomery, Jason Priestley, Josh Randall, David Sutcliffe, Eric Szmanda and Mary Tyler Moore. It was directed by Peter Werner.

Snow Wonder was filmed on location at Houmas House and around New Orleans.

Revenge of the Bridesmaids - 2010

When Abigail and Parker return from New York City to visit their home town, they discover that their best friend Rachel is a bridesmaid in the wedding of their childhood friend Caitlyn. Caitlyn is marrying Tony, who was Rachel's boyfriend until Caitlyn interfered. Abigail and Parker decide to run some interference of their own.

They manipulate Caitlyn and become bridesmaids so that they and Rachel can sabotage the wedding from the inside. With help from a police detective who happens to be a groomsman, the girls strive to ruin Caitlyn's wedding while dodging her controlling mother and hopefully reuniting Tony and Rachel.

The film starred Raven-Symoné (below), JoAnna Garcia Swisher (below), Beth Broderick and was directed by James Hayman.

Houmas House stood in for Belle Fontaine.

Loss, of a Teardrop Diamond - 2010

See St. Louis Plantation.

Love, Marriage, Wedding - 2011

A marriage counselor's life as a newlywed is turned upside down when she discovers her parents' happy marriage is unexpectedly headed for divorce. Determined to reconcile her parents for their 30th anniversary surprise party, she stops at nothing, plunging from one compromising situation to another. Dermot Mulroney directs the cast which includes Mandy Moore (above), Kellan Lutz (above), James Brolin, Jane Seymour, Michael Weston and Christopher Lloyd.

Houmas House hosted the on-screen wedding of Moore and Lutz.

LAKEVIEW/FAIRVIEW PLANTATION
East Feliciana Parish

The plantation was settled early in the 1800's by the East family who, bringing with them household goods and furniture to start a new home in Louisiana, came to the area from South Carolina. It was during the period soon after the United States gained possession of the territory when many others from the Atlantic seaboard came and made new homes here. Lakeview was built in 1830 by William East, son of the early pioneer. The house shows influence of his early Carolina background since it was built entirely of heart pine instead of cypress usually found in most Louisiana houses.

The curving driveway leads to the entrance where a wide gallery extends the length of the two-story house. The columns of the gallery are slender at the first-floor level and the gallery is enclosed by a plain balustrade. A deep slanting roof above gives some indication of the age of the structure. This type of architecture is different from most of Louisiana's houses built during the same period.

Lakeview, like many antebellum plantation houses, is situated near a small lake, from which the house and plantation derive the name. In the rear is an old building constructed of deep red brick. The clay used to bake the brick, it is believed, was dug from this lake nearby. Here the outside kitchen and dining room used in earlier days remain with much of its old-fashioned furnishings and equipment. Some early chairs and chests are yet retained there. The entire house is furnished with artistic antiques in harmony with the period in which the house was built.

Like other Feliciana plantations, Lakeview felt the sting of the invader during the War Between the States. It is believed that the columns of the front gallery may still contain bullets fired by the Union invaders.

The house has passed through a number of owners through the years: Charles East; Hezekial Burton Thompson; Dr. William Kernan Irvin and his wife Martha Octavia Gayden (who restored the home erasing all the scars of war) and Martha Gayden Yancey.

In 1966, the film **Alvarez Kelly** was shot on location at Lakeview/Fairview.

Alvarez Kelly - 1966

In *Alvarez Kelly*, William Holden and Richard Widmark star as a renegade adventurer and a reckless colonel, respectively. The drama features violent action and romantic intrigue, based on a true incident of the Civil War when Confederate cavalry fought a series of bloody battles in an effort to steal a huge herd of cattle from the Union army in order to feed the people of Richmond who were being starved into submission by General Grant. The film also starred Janice Rule, Patrick O'Neal, Victoria Shaw, Roger C. Carmel, and Richard Rust. It was directed by Edward Dmytryk.

The film was photographed on location in Louisiana after producer Sol Siegel discovered that there no longer was a Virginia circa 1864. Housing developments, power lines, roads and similar modern conveniences made filming "where the story actually happened" impossible. Specific Louisiana filming locations were around Clinton, Norwood and Baton Rouge, including Asphodel Plantation.

According to the *Alvarez Kelly* pressbook, the location shooting caused a number of problems. First, cast and crew were housed on the outskirts of Baton Rouge, which meant a 40-mile drive every morning. The weather was another issue. Extreme heat and humidity mingled with sudden thunderstorms.

Overcast days caused delays so that the color photography could match the lighting provided by sunny days. When Hurricane Betsy struck the area, cast and crew had to huddle in their motels while windows broke and trees and power lines toppled around them. Unfortunately, the hurricane did not wash away the insect population. The troupe continued to be bitten by mosquitoes, fire ants, bees and hornets. Even simple communications were difficult. One of the locations was 18 miles from the nearest telephone, which forced the crew to establish a courier service.

To promote the film, the Louisiana Tourist Commission prepared a 30x40" travel poster (right) which not only plugged the film but also some of the state's tourist

LAURA PLANTATION
St. James Parish

Guillaume Benjamin Demézière Duparc's sugar farming complex was originally called l'habitation Duparc, Years later, it was renamed the Laura Plantation. At its largest size, it was approximately 12,000 acres, which included properties amassed over time. In 1804, Duparc, a French naval veteran of the American Revolution, acquired the property. Duparc also acquired adjacent parcels from Acadians who had settled the land 20 years prior. Duparc's new farm was located on prime real estate, on unusually high and cleared ground. He placed his manor house squarely in the middle of the large Colapissa Indian village that had been on-site for over a century.

Construction of Duparc's manor house began in 1804 and was completed 11 months later. The work was executed by highly-skilled slaves, probably of Senegalese descent, in pre-fabricated methods, typical of early Louisiana vernacular structures. This "*maison principale*" was raised high above ground, resting on blue-gray glazed brick columns and walls, supported underground by an 8-foot deep pyramidal brick foundation. The cypress superstructure was inlaid with locally fired brick (*briquette-entre-pôteau*), plastered inside and stuccoed outside, with a brightly painted (red, ochre, green and pearl) exterior. This U-shaped structure totaled approx. 24,000 sq. ft. and had a 2,500 sq. ft. detached kitchen to its rear. At Duparc's death in 1808, the l'habitation consisted of 10 sizable buildings, including quarters for 17 slaves, a barn, warehouses and a small, rudimentary sugar mill.

Approx. 400 ft. behind the house was a road, going south, perpendicular to the river, lined on both sides with slave cabins, facing the road and stretching a distance of 3.5 miles. This was always referred to as the "back" of the plantation, where enslaved laborers resided, distant from the area nearer the river, called the "front."

In the decades before the Civil War, the slave quarters consisted of 69 cabins, communal kitchens, a slave infirmary, and several water wells stationed along the same road. One mile behind the manor house stood the sugarmill. The mill was surrounded, as everything else on the farm, by sugarcane fields.

Duparc was at the plantation for only 4 years, dying in 1808, just 3 years after the house was built. His daughter Elisabeth married into the Locoul family, and generations later, Laura Locoul Gore, for whom the plantation is named, inherited the plantation after moving to New Orleans. (Image on the right is of a costumed Laura). Four generations of women in the Duparc family ran the growing sugarcane plantation until Laura sold it in1891 to the family of Florian Waguespack, who were French-speaking Creoles of Alsatian descent.

The Waguespacks continued to farm sugarcane until 1981, when it was bought by a consortium of investors who planned to destroy the historic buildings and build a bridge across the Mississippi River at this site. The still-active earthquake fault below the historic site ruined their venture, and the land went into receivership until it was sold at auction in 1992 to the St. James Sugar Cooperative. In 1993, the old homestead was acquired by the Laura Plantation Company, a private enterprise, for the purpose of restoring the site and opening it to the public as a Creole cultural attraction.

In August, 2004, an electrical fire destroyed 80% of the Big House and, after a 3 -year restoration effort, the site was completely re-opened for tours.

In 2007, Laura Plantation was the subject of the documentary *Reconstructing Creole*.

Reconstructing Creole - 2007

In the summer of 2004, an electrical fire seriously damaged Laura Plantation, leaving behind only the original Creole structure of the house. This film weaves together the story of Laura, named for plantation daughter Laura Lecoul Gore, who grew up on the estate, which was run by her mother and grandmother, with the stories of those rebuilding the house she lived in. Laura's nineteenth-century story leads viewers through Louisiana Creole culture and its ideas of language, race, and heritage. Meanwhile, craftspeople working on the house confront the racial consequences of the plantation past, as some realize they may be related to the Senegambian slaves who built the home two hundred years ago. The film was directed by Jennifer John Block.

LAUREL VALLEY PLANTATION
Lafourche Parish

Settlement of the Bayou Lafourche region came late in the eighteenth century under Spanish direction. In 1763 Spain took control of the Louisiana colony from the French; soon thereafter, Spain tried to establish control over the sparsely populated province. Spain looked favorably on French Acadians recently expelled from Nova Scotia, primarily because they were hard working, experienced farmers. Spanish authorities allowed the Acadians to settle first on the lands above New Orleans. In the 1770's Acadians began to move down into Lafourche Parish, establishing farms side by side, along the bayou The farms averaged five arpents (one arpent equals 192 feet) front and four arpents deep.

The first permanent settler on the lands that would be called Laurel Valley was Etienne Boudreaux, an Acadian who received a land grant from Spanish authorities in the early 1770's. Boudreaux's grant included five arpents of land fronting Bayou Lafourche to a depth of forty arpents. Little is known about the activities of the family, but the 1810 census lists thirteen persons at the Boudreaux residence, nine males and four females. Etienne Boudreaux died in 1819, and the land was probably vacated by his sons, who married and established their own farms elsewhere in Lafourche Parish.

Joseph William Tucker, a young Mississippi planter established Laurel Valley Plantation. He cleared the land, expanded the acreage, constructed a mill and introduced sugar cane to its fields. He arrived in Lafourche Parish from Natchez near the end of 1831 and quickly settled on about 815 acres that he owned in partnership with Thomas Barnard, also a Natchez planter. Tucker bought out Barnard in 1832 and, over the next fifteen years, acquired nearly 5,000 additional arpents. These purchases included the fifteen front arpents which he purchased from the Boudreauxs on December 12, 1834, for the price of $35 for fifteen front arpents.

During this time, the plantation consisted of many buildings, including a 15-room home which he built for his 15-year-old wife Marceline Gaude. It was burned at the Battle of Lafourche Crossing during the Civil War. After the death of Joseph Tucker, Laurel Valley's operations came under the management of a cousin, Caleb, who married Joseph's widow in 1855. The Civil War seriously disrupted Laurel Valley's activities.

In 1862, union troops placed it under strict military supervision after they captured New Orleans. General Benjamin Butler issued an order subjecting the property of Louisianians who hereafter bore arms against the United States government to confiscation. Laurel Valley lost its loyalty status around 1863 after Caleb joined Confederate troops at Vicksburg.

Due to mounting debts, Laurel Valley was sold on March 7, 1872, to a Thibodaux resident, Clay Knobloch. But on the same day that Knobloch passed his sale he sold the plantation to William P. Tucker of Terrebonne Parish, another son of Joseph Tucker.

William managed the plantation for the next 21 months and through two grinding seasons. He gave up and sold to Samuel W. Hammond of New Orleans on December 12, 1873. Hammond held Laurel Valley for only seven months and sold his interest on July 10, 1874 to Burch A. Wormald, a Thibodaux resident.

In 1874 Burch A. Wormald acquired Laurel Valley and initiated modernization of the mill and construction of the double Creole quarters and a portion of the main house. The "Big House" structure is the largest and most prestigious on the plantation. The elaborately wainscoted central hall runs 84 feet and is 12 feet wide. The ceilings are 14 feet high. The front porch is characterized by ornamental Victorian carpentry. The building represented two major periods of construction. In 1884, Burch A. Wormald employed Andrew Downey, a New Orleans carpenter, to build a residence. The building would be completed during the Barker-Lepine years, primarily from 1903 to 1912.

In early 1892, Womald was unable to meet his indebtedness to W. J. Behan and H. Zuberbier and sold them Laurel Valley. On January 12, 1893, the plantation was sold to the partnership of Frank Barker and J. Wilson Lepine, Sr. Under their leadership, Laurel Valley became a general factory mill not only grinding its own cane but also that of tenants and adjoining farms. They built a narrow gauge railroad line and used barges on the bayou to haul cane. The plantation prospered until Lepine's death in 1926. His son J. Wilson Lepine, Jr. took over the management of the plantation. Laurel Valley Plantation has remained in the Lepine-McKee family for over 100 years.

Laurel Valley Plantation was listed on the National Register of Historic Places on March 24, 1978. The plantation, with its nearly 60 original structures including general store, schoolhouse, slave quarters and share cropper houses, has been a major draw to filmmakers.

Angel Heart - 1987

The film takes place in the 1950s. Harry Angel is a private investigator hired by a man named Louis Cyphre to locate a pop singer who reneged on a debt. Harry ventures into Harlem, the first step of an investigation that takes an unexpected and somber turn. Each time Harry makes contact with someone who might know the singer's whereabouts, he or she is killed in a horrible, ritualistic fashion. It appears that a Satanic cult seems to be the root of all the carnage. Harry solves the mystery not realizing that he had the answer all along -- even before Louis entered his office.

Angel Heart was written and directed by Alan Parker, and starred Mickey Rourke, Robert De Niro, and Lisa Bonet.

Laurel Valley Plantation provided some of the most intense scenes in **Angel Heart**, including the row of slave quarters (below).

A Gathering of Old Men - 1987

A Gathering of Old Men is a CBS made-for-TV movie which was released on video as **Murder on the Bayou**.

When a sheriff arrives at the home of a black man to investigate the murder of a white farmer in the deep south, he finds 18 elderly black men and Candy the white plantation owner, already there, each holding a recently fired rifle and claiming to be the killer.

The sheriff must present the murderer to his white friends to prevent them from practicing lynch justice. He doesn't want any unrest in his district, but becomes increasingly frustrated when interrogations, beatings and threats of violent retaliation do not intimidate the old men. Each one professes his guilt and all of them have a motive: the cruelty of the dead white man.

A Gathering of Old Men was based on the novel by Ernest J. Gaines. It starred Louis Gossett, Jr. (below), Richard Widmark, Holly Hunter, Joe Seneca and Will Patton and was directed by Volker Schlondorff .

Laurel Valley served as the setting for the film.

Three on a Match - 1987

When a naïve computer expert, a con artist and a lady's man end up in a Louisiana prison farm, they plot their escape and join forces on the outside. This made-for-TV movie starred Patrick Cassidy, David Hemmings, and Bruce A. Young and was directed by Donald P. Bellisario.

The film was shot on location at Laurel Valley Plantation.

Margaret Bourke White - 1989

Margaret Bourke White, a/k/a Double *Exposure: The Story of Margaret Bourke-White*, was a TNT made-for-TV movie based on the life of famed photojournalist Margaret Bourke-White who not only captured many of the definitive images of world history in the first half of the 20th century, but also was the first female photographer to risk her life covering the battlefields of World War II.

The film covers the period from the late 1920s through the 1930s and 1940s, when she was making a name for herself at *Life* Magazine. It also focuses on her relationship with acclaimed writer Erskine Caldwell and how she sacrificed that relationship for a career.

The movie stars Farrah Fawcett as Bourke-White, Frederic Forrest, David Huddleson, Jay Patterson, Mitch Ryan and was directed by Lawrence Schiller.

Margaret Bourke White was filmed at Laurel Valley Plantation and other Thibodaux locations.

Point of No Return - 1993

Maggie Hayward is a young, violent and unstable drug addict found guilty of murdering a police officer. She is sentenced to death by lethal injection. Her death is faked, and a secret government agent named Bob informs her that she is to become an assassin. She is given a makeover and training that transform her into a beautiful woman, and she is also trained as a killer. Her career as an assassin goes well at first. Then, after a mission goes awry, the agency sends in Victor, a "cleaner," to kill everyone and destroy the bodies.

The film was directed by John Badham and starred Bridget Fonda, Gabriel Byrne and Harvey Keitel. It is a remake of Luc Besson's 1990 film *Nikita*.

Some scenes were shot on location at Laurel Valley Plantation.

Interview with the Vampire - 1997

See Destrehan Plantation.

Old Man - 1997

This Hallmark Hall of Fame TV movie presents an adaptation of William Faulkner's short story about two lost souls who rediscover life and love. J.J. Taylor and fellow convicts are expected to help rescue survivors of a dangerous flood on the banks of the Mississippi (the "Old Man") in 1927.

J.J. sets off to find a woman caught up in a cypress snag, while the others attempt an escape. He is able to locate Addie, who is on the verge of giving birth, and they journey down the Mississippi together in a small boat. When the baby is born, J.J.'s humanity is rekindled and the woman, who has been abandoned by her husband, finds a compassionate friend who genuinely cares for her and her baby.

Old Man starred Jeanne Tripplehorn, Arliss Howard, and Leo Burmester and was directed by John Kent Harrison.

Laurel Valley Plantation and Alligator Bayou are the backdrops for the film.

A Lesson Before Dying - **1999**

In the 1940s South, an African-American man is wrongly accused of the killing of a white store owner. In his defense, his white attorney equates him with a lowly hog, to indicate that he did not have the sense to know what he was doing. He is convicted and sentenced to die. His godmother and the aunt of the local schoolteacher convince the schoolteacher to go to the convicted man's cell each day to try to reaffirm to him that he is not an animal but a man with dignity. The film is based on a novel by Ernest J. Gaines.

Joseph Sargent directed the film which starred Don Cheadle, Mekhi Phifer and Cicely Tyson.

Much of the HBO film was shot on Laurel Valley Plantation, including the slave cabins (below), the school building and the store. Filming was also done at Magnolia Plantation in Schriever.

Ray - **2004**

Ray is the story of the life and career of the legendary rhythm and blues musician Ray Charles, from his humble beginnings in the South, where he went blind at age seven, to his meteoric rise to stardom during the 1950s and 1960s. Directed by Taylor Hackford, the film starred Jamie Foxx, C. J. Sanders, Sharon Warren, Aretha Robinson, Kerry Washington, Regina King, Renee Wilson and Larenz Tate.

Laurel Valley Plantation served as the Ray Charles' childhood home in Greenville, Florida.

MADEWOOD PLANTATION
Assumption Parish

Built between 1840-48, Madewood Plantation House reflects the aspirations of its original owner, Colonel Thomas Pugh, a member of a prominent and wealthy Louisiana family.

Pugh arrived here with his two brothers from the tidewater region of North Carolina in 1818, just 15 years after Thomas Jefferson purchased Louisiana from Napoleon. The Pugh brothers snapped up property along the bayou and erected noble houses on their muddy lands.

Madewood was the manor house for the group of plantations that Pugh acquired in the 1830s and 40s, which eventually totaled some 10,000 acres. Sugar cane production brought economic prosperity to the area around Bayou Lafourche in the first part of the 19th century.

The home represents one of the finest and purest examples of the Greek Revival style architecture in a plantation home. In a grove of oaks and magnolias facing Bayou Lafourche, Pugh and his architect, Henry Howard, constructed a house whose classical splendor would surpass that of the neighboring plantations.

While Madewood is one of many plantations along the bayou, it stands out for its architectural grandeur, which is unique in its blending of its classical features with indigenous material.

The house is built of bricks made on the plantation, while the exterior is covered with stucco, scored to represent masonry blocks and painted white. The proportions are carefully determined, the six fluted Ionic columns rise two stories, with the central portion retaining the character of a Greek temple. Two one-story wings, echoing the predominant elements of the main house, complete the facade.

The interior contains 23 rooms, with floors of heart pine, doorframes and moldings of cypress, painted to resemble oak (or faux bois). Each doorway is signed by the artist, Cornealieus Hennessey. Elsewhere, the woodwork, including the cypress mantelpieces, has been painted to resemble marble or exotic woods.

The Civil War spared Madewood, but much of the grandeur had already departed with Thomas' death in 1852. His widow, Eliza Foley, was rumored to have saved Madewood from looting by advising a Union general that Thomas had been a Mason, as was the general.

After the war, Madewood passed through several families. Leon Godchaux bought the plantation in 1896 for $30,000. It was then acquired by Alcee F. Delaune and Henry Delaune.

In the second decade of the 20th century, Mr. and Mrs. R. L. Baker acquired the property and installed all the then-modern conveniences and adorned the ballroom with etched glass screens in the Art Nouveau style. The Baker's sold Madewood to Mr. Bronier Thibaut in 1946.

Naomi Marshall, a New Orleans native and prosperous businesswoman, purchased the property in 1964 for $75,000. The home was in serious disrepair and badly in need of a new roof. The Marshalls undertook a major restoration of the home, which was completed in 1978.

The property is now owned by the Marshall sons. It is open to the public daily and is the center for an annual arts festival and other cultural events.

The grounds today include the main house and attached kitchen, and in the rear, the carriage house, the Pugh family cemetery, Elmfield Cottage and the Madewood slave quarters.

Madewood Plantation and its grounds have appeared in a number of movies.

A Woman Called Moses - 1979

The 1978 made-for-TV mini series focused on the life of African American abolitionist and slave escape leader Harriet Tubman.

At the risk of recapture, Tubman helped organize the underground railroad. This enabled hundreds of enslaved African Americans to make their way to the freedom of the Northern states. Adding to the tension are Harriet's frequent epileptic fainting spells.

The film starred Cecily Tyson as Tubman, Will Geer, Robert Hooks and James Wainwright. Orson Welles narrates this adaptation of Marcy Heidish's novel which was directed by Paul Wendkos.

The photo below is a movie still featuring Cecily Tyson as Harriet Tubman. The real Harriet Tubman appears in the inset.

Madewood Plantation served as the Broadas home.

Sister Sister - 1987

In this thriller, sisters Charlotte and Lucy Bonnard reside in the Louisiana home left to them by their parents. As Charlotte cares for her troubled younger sister, the two make a living by renting out rooms in the huge, gloomy mansion. However, when businessman Matt Rutledge comes to stay, he stumbles across a number of the Bonnards' dark secrets that were best left hidden.

Sister Sister was directed and co-written by Bill Condon. The film starred Eric Stoltz, Jennifer Jason Leigh, and Judith Ivey.

Madewood Plantation was the setting for the film's plantation house turned bed and breakfast. Other scenes were shot at the Greenwood Plantation.

Cigarettes and Nylons - 2010

In this French-made TV movie, three women are in a foreign land. They hardly speak the language, don't know the customs, but vow to be good wives to young men they barely know.

The year is 1946. The foreign land is the United States. In WWII, during brief encounters and stolen moments, 6,500 American recruits married French girls even while fighting their way to Paris and beyond. An overwhelmed U.S. Army set up "cigarette" camps — Camp Chesterfield, Camp Lucky Strike — to "Americanize" the brides before shipping them to the care of in-laws they'd never met. *Cigarettes & Nylons* follows three young women through hope and disillusionment, love and heartbreak, to a time when even as the world was burning, young hearts were set aflame.

The film starred Adelaide Leroux, Salome Stevenin, Melodie Richard, Billy Slaughter, Jean-Captiste Fonck, Jessie Terrebonne, James Yeargin. Director: Fabrice Cazeneuve. It was directed by Fabrice Cazeneuve and was produced by Louisiana filmmakers Michelle Benoit & Glen Pitre.

Madewood Plantation was one of the filming locations for the film.

MAGNOLIA PLANTATION
Schriever, Louisiana

Constructed in 1858 along Little Bayou Black, the frame, two-story Greek Revival residence was built by Thomas Ellis. It was constructed of cypress cut by slaves and sits among the flowering trees from which it takes its name.

The first floor front is of plastered brick, the rest of frame construction. The interior boasts a rosewood staircase. The kitchen is in a separate building; another outbuilding, constructed of double brick walls between which charcoal has been tightly packed, houses the cistern and was designed to keep the water cool at all times.

There are fourteen foot ceilings and a central hall fourteen feet wide. In addition, most of the major rooms are twenty-five feet square. On the ground story there are two rooms on the north side of the hall which connect by means of massive sliding doors. South of the hall are four rooms which terminate in a single story rear wing. The five-bay facade features a two-story gallery with heavy Doric posts upstairs and down.The gallery terminates with a heavy entablature and a denticular cornice. The sides and rear of the house are trimmed with Greek Revival details.

The stair hall is separated from the central hall by an elliptical arch resting upon cast plaster consoles. The stair hall terminates in a 180 degree curving wall similar to an apse. The thickly proportioned staircase follows the curve of the rear wall in a graceful ascent. Instead of a single newel, the stair terminates in a 360 degree curving balustrade. The stair hall is its rear exit where both the door and the door frame are steamed to exactly conform to the curve of the rear wall.

The interior cornices are heavy and richly molded. Most of the original mantels survive. On the ground story the three original mantels are of white marble in the Rococo Revival style. The two other mantels on the ground floor date from the late-nineteenth or early-twentieth centuries. On the upper story the mantels are of wood and feature a relatively simple aedicule style. Most of the major ground story rooms feature Rococo Revival ceiling medallions.

Ellis's daughter Eliza (left) married Confederate general Braxton Bragg here. A productive sugar plantation, during the Civil War, Magnolia was used as a hospital by Federal troops. It is said that the soldiers used the owner's grand piano as a food trough for horses.

Captain John Jackson Shaffer bought the property in 1874 and it is still occupied by direct descendents.

Magnolia Plantation House is locally significant in the area of architecture as probably the finest example among the few surviving Greek Revival residences in Terrebonne Parish. Terrebonne Parish developed during the first half of the nineteenth century as a center for the growing and refining of sugar. Like most of Louisiana's sugar parishes, the parish's economy boomed in the thirty years or so prior to the Civil War. As a result, during this period a large number of Greek Revival plantation houses were built which represented something of an architectural "flowering" for the parish.

The importance of Magnolia within this context can be illustrated by examining the census schedules of 1860. On the eve of the Civil War, there were forty-four large slaveholdings (i.e., fifty or more slaves) in the parish. Of these, the average size per slaveholding was 115.2 and only six involved individuals who did not reside in the parish. In addition, there were undoubtedly numerous slaveholdings of less than 50.

Given the above, it is clear that there must have been numerous Greek Revival plantation houses and cottages in Terrebonne Parish on the eve of the Civil War (probably at least sixty). However, as far as the State Historic Preservation Office can determine, there are only six remaining examples. Consequently Magnolia is of special importance in the architectural heritage of the parish.

In addition, of the six which do survive, Magnolia is probably the finest. It is one of only two which possess a two story front gallery. Moreover, it has high style features seldom found on plantation houses. These include: (1) the cast-iron balustrades; (2) the Rococo Revival marble mantels: (3) the highly unusual curving rear wall of the stair hall with its steam fitted door and frame; and (4) the elliptical arch in the central hall with its cast plaster consoles.

The Magnolia Plantation has been featured in several films.

Crazy in Alabama - 1999

Crazy in Alabama marks the directorial debut of Antonio Banderas (right). The film is based on a screenplay by Mark Childress, based on his novel of the same name.

The story involves an abused wife who heads to California to become a movie star while her nephew back in Alabama has to deal with a racially-motivated murder involving a corrupt sheriff.

The film starred Melanie Griffith, David Morse, Meat Loaf, Cathy Moriarty, Lucas Black and Rod Steiger.

Magnolia Plantation served as Meemaw's home (below) in the film.

A Lesson Before Dying - 1999

Magnolia Plantation serves as the Guidry home. See Laurel Valley Plantation.

Best of Me - 2014

Based on the bestselling novel by acclaimed author Nicholas Sparks, *The Best of Me* tells the story of Dawson and Amanda, two former high school sweethearts who find themselves reunited after 20 years apart, when they return to their small town for the funeral of a beloved friend.

Their bittersweet reunion reignites the love they've never forgotten, but soon they discover the forces that drove them apart twenty years ago live on, posing even more serious threats today.

Spanning decades, this epic love story captures the enduring power of our first true love, and the wrenching choices we face when confronted with elusive second chances.

The film starred James Marsden, Michelle Monaghan, Luke Bracey and Liana Liberato and was directed by Michael Hoffman.

Magnolia Plantation serves as the home of Amanda.

The photo below is of Marsden, Monaghan and director Hoffman discussing a scene on location at Magnolia.

MYRTLES PLANTATION
West Feliciana Parish

The drama of The Myrtles began in 1796 when General David Bradford, also known as "Whiskey Dave" of the Whiskey Rebellion, fled the United States to avoid arrest and imprisonment. General Bradford arrived at Bayou Sara, then a Spanish Colony, and obtained a land grant of 650 acres from the Baron de Corondelet to begin a new life. A wealthy judge and businessman from Washington County, Pennsylvania, Bradford showed interest in the area before the conclusion of the unsuccessful Whiskey Rebellion forced him to settle there. Bradford built the plantation that was known as Laurel Grove (later named "the Myrtles") in 1797.

The house is a broad, low, rambling frame mansion with a clapboard exterior and was built in two halves. The first half, which was built in 1796, forms the western six bays of the main façade. These were increased in size due to mid-19th-century restoration, when the house also received a southward extension that almost doubled its size. The unusually long gallery is supported by an exceptional cast-iron railing of elaborate grape-cluster design. It is the interior detailing, however, which is perhaps the most important feature of the Myrtles Plantation. Most of the ground floor rooms have fine marble, arched mantles in the Rococo Revival style, with central console keystones or cartouches. Most of the rooms have plaster-ceiling medallions, no two of which are the same.

Bradford died in 1808, and in 1820, his widow sold the land to her son-in-law, Judge Clark Woodruff, a lawyer and friend of Andrew Jackson. In 1834 Woodruff sold it to Ruffin Gray Stirling. Stirling and his wife, Mary Catherine Cobb, undertook an extensive remodeling of the house. When completed, the new house was nearly double the size of the former building, and its name was changed to The Myrtles. The Stirlings had nine children, but five of them died young. Stirling died in 1854 and left the plantation to his wife.

In 1865, Mary Cobb hired William Drew Winter to help manage the plantation as her lawyer and agent. Winter was married to Mary Cobb's daughter, Sarah Stirling. Sarah and William Winter lived at the Myrtles and had six children, one of whom (Kate Winter) died from typhoid at the age of three. Although the Winters were forced to sell the plantation in 1868, they were able to buy it back two years later.

In 1871, William Winter was shot on the porch of the house, possibly by a man named E.S. Webber, and died within minutes. Sarah remained at the Myrtles' with her mother and siblings until 1878, when she died. Mary Cobb died in 1880, and the plantation passed to Stephen, one of her sons. The plantation was heavily in debt, however, and Stephen sold it in 1886 to Oran D. Brooks. Brooks sold it in 1889, and the house changed hands several times until 1891, when it was purchased by Harrison Milton Williams.

Over the next several decades, the land was split up and owned by various Williams heirs. In the 1950s, the property surrounding the house had been divided among the Williams heirs and the house itself was sold to Marjorie Munson, an Oklahoma widow.

The property was transferred a few more times and in the 1970's, Arlin Dease and Mr. & Mrs. Robert Ward purchased the property. They did not own the home for very long. James and Frances Myers were the next owners. Believing the home was haunted, it began to be featured in books and magazines about haunted houses. Frances, publishing as Francis Kermeen, wrote a book about the Myrtles and its supposed haunting.

The home currently is owned by John & Teeta Moss and is now a bed & breakfast. Historical and mystery tours are also offered. The plantation house was listed on the National Register of Historic Places in 1978.

The TV movie *Long Hot Summer* was filmed in part at The Myrtles.

The Long Hot Summer - 1985

The Long Hot Summer was a 1985 TV movie based on the 1958 theatrical film of the same name-which, in turn, was based on two William Faulkner short stories. Ben, a southern drifter, is under suspicion as a "barn burner." He secures a job at the Mississippi mansion of town-boss Will Varner. Varner's daughter Noel and daughter-in-law Eula vie for the handsome Ben's attention, while the patriarch's weakling son Jody seethes. Originally aired on October 6 and 7, 1985, the film starred film Don Johnson, Cybill Shepherd, and Jason Robards.

The Long Hot Summer was filmed in part at The Myrtles. The Myrtles is touted as "one of America's most haunted homes", supposedly inhabited by at least 12 ghosts. The film crew reported that when they moved furniture for a scene, someone would move it back to its original places! No one had been reported in the room at the time. They had to move the furniture several times in order to get the shots they needed, and were glad to be finished.

NOTTOWAY PLANTATION
Iberville Parish

The Nottoway Plantation House, known as "the white castle of Louisiana," is one of the largest antebellum plantation houses in the south, composed of 64 rooms, seven staircases, and five galleries.

This 53,000-square foot plantation home, constructed by John Hampden Randolph in 1858, is a fine example of an antebellum home. Randolph, whose father had come from Virginia in 1820, purchased the area in 1841. (Randolph, wife Emily and children below).

Nottoway sits about 200 feet behind the Mississippi River Levee surrounded by oaks, magnolias, pecan trees, and sweet olives. Nottoway House is distinctive for being an essentially Italianate Style plantation house built in an era dominated by Greek Revival architecture. Nottoway contains an elegant, half-round portico as the side gallery follows the curve of the large ballroom bay window.

Nottoway's thin Italianate pillars stretch vertically to touch all of its three levels, extending from the house's one-story brick base to the paramount height of the third-story made of wooden frame. From the front gallery the Mississippi River is in view. The interior of Nottoway is white in color, including Corinthian columns, lace curtains, carved marble mantels and even the floor, creating an elegant environment

In 1860 Nottoway Plantation encompassed 6,200 acres and Randolph, the builder and owner of the property during that time, owned 155 African-Americans that worked his sugarcane plantation as slaves. When Randolph was ready to build his house, he went to New Orleans and asked various architects to submit designs, and chose Henry Howard's.

The grounds of Nottoway were occupied by both Union and Confederate troops during the Civil War, and the castle was fired upon several times by Northern gunboats. Nottoway was actually saved from one attack by a young Northern officer on board a gunboat. He had been graciously entertained at the plantation's garden parties and balls prior to the war, and recognized the castle from the Mississippi River. He called for a cease-fire, sparing the home from damage in that battle. But, the plantation grounds were not immune to shelling and canons during the war. By 1863, Mrs. Randolph had to give the Oath of Loyalty to the Union in order to keep Nottoway.

The Randolphs held onto the house through the Civil War and Reconstruction. John Randolph died in 1883.

In 1889, Mrs. Randolph sold the mansion to New Orleans natives V.B Dugas and Desire Landry for $50,000. Mrs. Randolph divided the money equally among the surviving children and herself.   The firm of Dugas and Landry sold Nottoway to M. Hanlon Sons in 1909 for $63,000.00.

In 1913, Dr. Whyte Owen of White Castle bought Nottoway at a sheriff's sale for $54,000. In 1980, Mrs. Odessa Owen, Dr. Owen's daughter-in-law, sold Nottoway to Arlin Dease for $270,000, with stipulation that she could live in the house until her death.

In July 1980, Nottoway's doors were opened for the first time to the public for touring. Mr. Dease transformed the plantation home into a bed & breakfast, special events and tourist venue. In 1985, Sir Paul Ramsey of Australia purchased Nottoway from Arlin Dease. Sir Ramsey passed away in 2014.

Nottoway Plantation was featured in the following movies.

Louisiana - **1984**

See Greenwood Plantation.

Everybody's All American - **1988**

Spanning the mid-1950s to the early 1980s, the lives of three longtime friends, an All-American football hero, his college sweetheart and his devoted nephew, remain intertwined for a quarter century in this Taylor Hackford directed drama based on Frank Deford's novel.

The film starred Dennis Quaid (below), Jessica Lange (below) and Timothy Hutton.

Nottoway Plantation provided the backdrop for the Magnolia Queen crowning of 1963.

Hard Target - **1993**

A down-on-his-luck New Orleans merchant sailor uses his high-powered martial arts skills to battle a sadistic band of hunters who prey on homeless veterans in a deadly safari game. His quest begins when he comes to the rescue of a young woman whose father was a recent victim of the killers.

The film starred Jean-Claude Van Damme (next page), Lance Henrikson, Yancy Butler and Wilfred Brimley. It was directed by John Woo (next page)

Hard Target features scenes filmed at Nottoway Plantation.

Heaven's Prisoners - **1995**

Based on the novel by James Lee Burke, the film follows an alcoholic New Orleans cop who leaves the big city to settle into life on the bayou with his wife Annie. There they witness a small plane crash in the Gulf and rescue a small Salvadoran girl who they unofficially adopt. Though the crash looks accidental, Robicheaux's instincts tell him otherwise and he starts an investigation which leads him to a local organized crime syndicate headed by Bubba Rocque, his old high school buddy.

Heaven's Prisoners was directed by Phil Joanou and starred Alec Baldwin, Kelly Lynch, Mary Stuart Masterson and Eric Roberts.

Nottaway Plantation served as the drug pin's bayou mansion (above).

OAK ALLEY PLANTATION
St. James Parish

In July 1830, Valcour Aime purchased the area known as "Section 7," that would later become Oak Alley. He used it for planting sugarcane, a crop that would propel him to wealth.

In May 1836, Jacques Telesphore Roman (right) acquired the property. Originally named Bon Sejour, Oak Alley was built in 1837-39 by George Swainey for Roman, brother of Andre Roman who was twice governor of Louisiana. Joseph Pilie, Roman's father-in-law, was an architect and is thought to have provided the design of Oak Alley. It took three years to complete the house.

Oak Alley's most distinguishing architectural feature is a full peripteral (free-standing) colonnade of 28 colossal Doric columns. Placing it at the head of the allee' of Oaks, Jacques built his home in the fashionable Greek Revival style. Bricks were made on-site, but slate for the roof, glass for the windows, and marble for the dining room floor had to be shipped in by steamboat. It was an extremely laborious and time-consuming endeavor, accomplished entirely with slave labor.

Equally significant is the impressive double row of giant live oak trees which form the oak alley, about 800 feet long, from which the property derived its present name. Planted before the house was constructed in 1837, this formal planting is a historic landscape design long recognized for its beauty.

An important event in American horticultural history occurred in the winter of 1846-47 when Antoine, a slave gardener at Oak Alley, first successfully grafted pecan trees. His work resulted in the first named variety, Centennial, and the first commercial pecan orchard at nearby Anita Plantation.

Jacques Telesphore Roman was never a healthy man, and in April of 1848, he died of Tuberculosis at age 48. He was extremely particular in his will: placing his brother A.B in charge of the plantation finances, forbidding the sale of slaves, any removal of the pecan grove, and lastly requested his children be educated and reside in St. James, and not in New Orleans--the city he so despised. Jacques' will left the estate in portions to his widow Celini and Henri (left), Louise and Octavie, with the intent that it would be operated jointly. However, Henri purchased his sister's and mother's percentages, after much negotiating and bitter disputes, particularly with Louise.

By May of 1865, by the time of Lee's Surrender at Appomattox Courthouse, Henri Roman had all but given up on Oak Alley. Some "freed men" remained, working as paid laborers, but the economy was nonexistent and infrastructure equally fragile.

In March of 1966, Henri signed Oak Alley back to his family. The Civil War and Celina's lingering debt were too much for Henri to overcome. Rather than accomplishing his goal of completely buying out his family's shares in the plantation, he now owed them immense sums of money. In addition to his mother and sister Louise, Henri indebted to his Uncle Valcour, and even his own wife, Therese. In today's figures, the amount he owed his family would have been slightly over $3 million.

Unable to retain the plantation, and Celina having passed away, Valcour, Octavie and Louise put the estate up for auction. In December of 1866, John Armstrong, a businessman from New Orleans, bought the plantation at an auction from the Whitney Bank. Over an 18-year period, other owners controlled the plantation and used it for agricultural purposes.

Antoine Sobral, a native of Portugul, purchased Oak Alley at a sheriff's sale in 1882 and brought the property back to a proper family home for his wife and children. Under this new ownership, the plantation flourished, and Sobral was accepted as one of the area's most outstanding figures, both as a proud veteran of the Confederacy and as a generous and wise gentleman who commanded respect from all who knew him. His reign had lasted 24 years when, in 1905, poor health and advancing years convinced him that he should accept an offer to sell Oak Alley.

On February 3, 1905, Antoine Sobral sold Oak Alley to the partnership of Etienne O. Hotard and J. D. Pittman. On January 20, 1911, the partnership of Etienne Ozeme Hotard & J.B. Pittman sold Oak Alley to Ephriam Rosenberg for debts. Hotard retained the plantation store for three more years. The operation of the store passed to the hands of his sons.

Rosenberg, who was from New Orleans, purchased the plantation as an investment. Rosenberg remained in New Orleans and leased the lands for rice production. The lessee(s) may have lived in parts of the mansion, but left sometime in 1912.

On December 28, 1917, Rosenberg sold Oak Alley to Jefferson Davis Hardin, Jr. The first resident in decades, Hardin began to make much needed repairs, including repairing the roof. However, bad growing seasons and the economic downturn after World War I placed the Hardins in an impossible financial position.

The final straw for the Hardins was when one of their cows caused a train derailment on the back end of the plantation. Losing their case, they were forced to give up the plantation they had tried so hard to restore. On April 19, 1924, Jefferson Davis Hardin, Jr. signed the property over to Whitney Bank.

On June 4, 1925, Alice Teplitz purchased the property from Whitney Bank. Then on July 22, 1925,Teplitz sold the plantation to Andrew and Josephine Stewart (right)

The house was in a state of deterioration. The Stewarts hired architect Richard Koch to conduct an extensive restoration. The pale pink of the plastered columns and walls and the blue green of the louvered shutters and gallery railing were color choices of Mrs. Stewart at that time. Square in plan, the interior has a central hall from front to rear on both floors. At each end of both halls the doors have broad fanlights and sidelights framed with slim, fluted colonnettes. Rooms at the first floor rear were partitioned and adapted to modern uses at the time of restoration in the 1920s.

On June 28, 1995 live oaks that form the Alee leading from the river to the Big House were inducted into the Live Oak Society. Each tree was given a name honoring individuals who left a lasting impression on this national historic landmark.

Oak Alley has been a favorite filming location for movie and television producers.

Hush, Hush Sweet Charlotte - 1964

See Houmas House Plantation.

Dixie: Changing Habits - 1982

Dixie's life changes completely after the prostitution ring she runs is raided. She is arrested and sentenced to spend time in a convent. Though she is there to learn, she ends up teaching the Mother Superior and the others a thing or two about running a successful business. By the story's end, Dixie has learned to respect herself.

This CBS TV movie starred Suzanne Pleshette, Cloris Leachman, John Considine and Geraldine Fitzgerald and was directed by George Englund.

It was filmed entirely on location at Oak Alley Plantation and the French Quarter in New Orleans.

Netherworld - 1992

Netherworld is the story of Corey Thornton, whose life takes a major turn when he inherits a Louisiana plantation from his estranged father. Upon arriving at the massive home, he discovers that a secretive cult is using winged creatures to raise the dead to do their bidding. Through instructions left for him, Corey learns of his father's bizarre plan and wish to be resurrected from the grave. With the help of a local prostitute and voodoo temptress, Corey learns the ways of black magic. Now, haunted by his father and experiencing bizarre illusions, Corey is about to enter the world beyond his own imagination.

Netherworld was written and directed by David Schmoelle and starred Michael Bendetti, Denise Gentile, Holly Floria, Robert Sampson and Robert Burr.

Oak Alley was featured as the plantation which forms the backdrop for the film. (right)

Something to Talk About - *1995*

Grace is managing her father's riding stable when she discovers that her husband Eddie is having an affair with another woman. After confronting him in the middle of the night on the streets of their small home town, she decides to stay at her sister's house to decide what she is going to do about her marriage. To her surprise, she also discovers that people around her suggest that she forgive and forget instead of making an issue out of it. She starts to question the authority of everyone, especially her father's, thus causing a stir in her parent's marriage, too. Julia Roberts, Dennis Quaid, Robert Duvall, Gena Rowlands and Kyra Sedgwick starred in the film. It was directed by Lasse Hallstrom.

Oak Alley was featured in some of the film's scenes.

Primary Colors - *1998*

Mike Nichols directed this film adaptation from the 1996 bestseller by "Anonymous" (Joe Klein), who fictionalized Bill Clinton's first presidential campaign. In the New Hampshire primary, Governor Jack Stanton convinces Henry Burton, grandson of a respected civil rights pioneer, to become his deputy campaign manager. Stanton's smart wife Susan always comes through with public support for her philandering husband. Problems during the New Hampshire primary include charges of adultery. Stanton's staff brings in an old family friend, lesbian Libby Holden, to clean up dirt. Stanton, a strong debater, moves on to Florida and New York. When one opposing candidate drops dead of a heart attack, he's replaced by Florida's Governor Fred Picker, but Holden holds the key to the skeleton in Picker's closet.

John Travolta (below), Emma Thompson, Adrian Lester (below), Kathy Bates and Larry Hagman star.

Oak Alley served as Governor Fred Picker's mansion (below).

Midnight Bayou - 2009

Harvard-educated lawyer Declan Fitzpatrick fell in instant love with Manet Hall, a Louisiana bayou estate he first saw when riding with college friends. When he learns it is for sale, he buys the home from the destitute owner, Odette Simone, who lives in a cabin nearby.

Local legends claim that the house is haunted, and shortly after Declan moves in he begins hearing voices and seeing things. Declan is also distracted by an undeniable attraction to Lena Simone, Odette's granddaughter.

While living in the house, Declan begins to have visions from a century past and details of events that took place in the mansion. With the help of Odette, Declan and Lena realize that they are inextricably linked with Manet Hall, and uncover a shocking secret that has been hidden there for more than 100 years.

This made-for-TV movie was directed by Ralph Hemecker and starred Jerry O'Connell, Lauren Stamile, and Faye Dunaway. The film is based on the Nora Roberts novel of the same name.

Oak Alley stars as Manet Hall (below).

OAKLAND PLANTATION
Natchitoches Parish

Oakland Plantation, part of the Cane River Creole National Historical Park, originally known as Bermuda, was begun by Jean Pierre Emmanuel Prudhomme on a tract of land granted to him by the Spanish government in 1789. Prudhomme and his wife Marie Catherine Lambre Prudhomme completed building Oakland in 1821.

He quickly built a fortune, vastly increasing his land holdings. Oakland was one of the first plantations to grow cotton on a large scale. At the time of his death in 1845, he held 104 enslaved people. Emmanuel's estate passed into the hands of his descendants, who continued to develop and expand the plantation. The Prudhomme land was split in 1868 between two heirs, Jacques Alphonse and Pierre Emmanuel. Jacques kept the land on the west side of the river, including the Main House and the area now considered Oakland Plantation. Pierre took all of the lands on the east side of the river and renamed his plantation Atahoe.

Though Oakland contains a fine example of a raised Creole plantation Main House, even more important are the 27 historic outbuildings still standing on the property. This rare wealth of buildings allows visitors to more completely understand life on a plantation.

Prior to the Civil War, large plantations often were more like small villages than farms. Though plantations focused on producing cash crops such as rice, sugarcane, tobacco or cotton, it was necessary for them to also grow food crops and raise poultry and livestock to support their large populations. A portion of the fields was often reserved for corn, potatoes, or other staple foods. Enslaved laborers were usually allowed to tend small personal gardens in their free time. Chickens, cattle, hogs and turkeys were raised by most plantations.

It was popular in the Cane River region to construct special buildings known as pigeonniers in which to raise pigeons. These birds would be eaten and their eggs would be harvested. Oakland Plantation has many remaining outbuildings that were used in food production. A corn crib is still extant, as is a cattle corral and dipping vat. Several buildings devoted to poultry production remain, including a hen house, fattening pen, turkey shed and two pigeonniers.

Oakland Plantation continued to be passed down from one generation of Prudhommes to another and parts of it are still farmed today. The Prudhomme family sold the core of Oakland Plantation to the National Park Service in 1997, and the last family left the land in 1999. It is now one of the two units of Cane River Creole National Historical ParK. Cane River Creole National Historical Park is in the process of restoring Oakland Plantation to its appearance circa 1860. Its goal is to portray Oakland as a working plantation and offer insight into the everyday lives of all of the people whose lives centered around this fertile ground for 200 years. Oakland Plantation was declared a National Historic Landmark in 2001.

The plantation was used as a backdrop in John Ford's 1959 movie *The Horse Soldiers*.

The Horse Soldiers - 1959

The Horse Soldiers was loosely based on an historical event during the Civil War. A former Illinois music teacher, Union colonel Benjamin H. Grierson, was ordered to take 1,700 men on a cavalry raid from the Tennessee border through Mississippi to destroy railroad supply lines, bridges and commissaries between April 17 and May 2, 1863.

The film starred John Wayne, William Holden, Constance Towers (right), Hoot Gibson and was directed by John Ford.

Oakland Plantation served as Hannah Hunter's Greenbrier home (above).

OAKLAWN MANOR
Natchitoches Parish

The saga of this lovely home begins with an Irishman named Alexander Porter (right). Porter arrived in the United Sates in 1801 at the young age of 16, having fled Ireland after his father's execution by the English during the Irish Rebellion of 1798. With his uncle and his brother James, Porter originally settled in Nashville, Tennessee, where he studied law and was admitted to the Tennessee Bar in 1807.

For two years, he served as a practicing attorney in Nashville. During that time, General Andrew Jackson, a family friend, advised Porter to move farther south to the territories of Louisiana or Mississippi. It was there, claimed the general, that Porter would find great success; for young men with such an education would be in high demand.

In 1809, taking General Jackson's advice, Alexander Porter found his new home in the Teche Country of Louisiana and quickly won the trust and friendship of the people there. Two years later, he was elected as a representative of Attakapas Parish to serve on the committee overseeing the creation of the Louisiana State Constitution.

His public career prospered. After Louisiana was admitted into the Union in 1812, Porter served in the lower house of the State Legislature for two years and then as an Associate Justice for the Louisiana Supreme Court for twelve years.

During the early years of Porter's public life, he began his work on Oaklawn Manor. In 1812 he began purchasing property along the Bayou Teche in St. Mary Parish until he owned thousands of acres along both sides of the Bayou. His sugar plantation grew immensely successful, and by 1840 Porter owned additional assets valued at roughly $100,000.

He married Evalina Baker, the daughter of Joshua Baker, in Franklin during the month of July 1815. Unfortunately, Porter's beloved Evalina died shortly after the birth of their second daughter, Anne, in 1819, and the couple's first daughter, also named Evalina, lived but for a short while. Porter's maiden sister assumed the responsibilities of caring for the young Anne and the household.

The Greek Revival mansion was built in 1837. It is constructed of brick from the surrounding soil, almost a fortress with its 20 inch thick walls. The white-stuccoed brick house has identical porticoes front and back, with six full-height Tuscan columns and a pediment ventilated by a small window. Both floors of the house are identical in plan, with two rooms on each side of a central hall

Poor health plagued the Porter family and saw an end to happier days. Porter's daughter Anne, no longer able to travel, passed away shortly after her marriage to Mr. Alston of South Carolina, leaving no heirs. Her father's death was not long in coming. Alexander Porter, the visionary of Oaklawn and popular statesman, died in 1844 at the age of 59. James Porter inherited his brother's estate and moved his family from a smaller plantation in West Baton Rouge Parish. James, much like his brother, succumbed to poor health. He died in 1849, bequeathing Oaklawn to his wife, Mary Walton Porter. At the time of James's death, the plantation and its remaining assets were valued at over $260,000.

Following the Civil War, the house was solely attended by Mrs. Walton Porter and her two daughters. With no slaves and few servants, the Porter women were unable to continue raising the fields of sugar cane, the only cash crop of the area. Consequently, when a wealthy New Yorker offered to buy the plantation, the ladies had little choice but to accept. In 1925 Captain Clyde Arthur Barbour acquired Oaklawn as a home for him and his wife, Jennie. Captain Barbour set about restoring Oaklawn manor to her former days of glory. Two years later, after carefully recreating the gardens and refurbishing the manor, the Barbours opened to the public a restored and newly resplendent Oaklawn Manor.

The Barbours also understood the importance of the oak trees which spread over the estate but had been long suffering from years of neglect. With the help of laborers, the family planted over one hundred twelve-year-old live oaks in the 1930's and brought in tree surgeons to revive the older, ailing trees. By chaining the limbs together to withstand the strong winds of hurricane seasons and carefully pruning away the dead limbs, the tree surgeons were able to save many of the beautiful old trees which had been standing for well over a hundred years.

Unfortunately, Captain Barbour passed away in 1930; but his widow continued to live there for nearly thirty years. The Barbours' daughter, Lucile married a man from Chicago, Illinois, who fell in love with Oaklawn Manor, and the two returned to live there permanently in the 1950's.

Lucile and Thomas J. Holmes, II, devoted their life to continuing the restoration of their beloved Oaklawn, opening the manor to the public and educating visitors about the history of their home. In 1963, Tom and Lucie sold Oaklawn to George B. Thomson, a young man form Crowley, Louisiana and a graduate of Duke University.

George and his wife, Mary Beth, together with interior designer Ernest Nereaux of New Iberia, set about refurbishing the manor. They combined the beauty of Oaklawn's past and the luxuries of present day. First, they completely rewired the house and installed air conditioning which would help preserve the antiques in the home from Louisiana's intense heat and humidity. To brighten the home's appearance, they painted the exterior - a daunting, yet rewarding, task that required 500 gallons of white paint. In addition, the Thomsons redecorated and insulated the newly dressed rooms with draperies lined with heavy cloth to keep out the hot summer sun. Lastly, they added the beautiful old furnishings that they had collected over the years. The result was a stunning facelift on a plantation worthy of great appreciation and admiration, as evidenced by its renewed popularity with all those who visited the historic home.

All was not easy for the new owners and their Oaklawn, however. Just one year after the Thomsons moved in, hurricane Hilda struck hard, costing the lives of 44 cedars along the property's Cedar Walk. The Thomson family sought refuge in the manor, propping furniture against the large wooden doors to prevent the storm from blowing through the structure. As the family waited out the storm, they could hear the chimneys crumbling from the onslaught of the torrential hurricane winds and rain. The Thomsons emerged unscathed, but their lovely home once again needed repairs. The following year, hurricane Betsy caused additional damage, although no major losses resulted.

In 1978, George and Mary Beth Thomson sold Oaklawn to a group of Arkansas investors and moved into the town of Franklin, where they currently reside. Later, the investor group made many changes to the estate, including dividing 40 acres of Oaklawn land and developing a subdivision of large homes along the property line. Oaklawn was bought and sold again, until she was back on the market as a result of financial problems

In 1985, M.J. " Mike" Foster Jr. surprised his wife, Alice, with the keys to what would become their new most beloved home just outside Franklin, Louisiana, Foster's hometown.Oaklawn Manor, with its 35 sprawling acres of oak-filled terrain, was home at first sight for the soon-to-be state senator (and, years later, Louisiana governor) and his wife. Complete with many of its original furnishings, the plantation was well-preserved.

Shortly after moving to Oaklawn, the governor discovered the back gates among a pile of rubbish that had been discarded. He quickly removed the gates from the pile and, after cleaning them off, returned them to their original assignment around the grounds of the manor. Their addition echoes the original days of Oaklawn, when they stood protecting and adorning the property.

Oaklawn Manor is listed on the National Register of Historic Places.

In 1975, the film *Drowning Pool* was filmed on location at Oaklawn.

Drowning Pool - 1975

Paul Newman reprised his role as Lew Harper, a private detective first introduced in the film *Harper*.   In this film, based on Ross Macdonald's novel *The Drowning Pool*, Harper is hired by an old flame, socialite Iris Devereaux, to investigate her philandering husband. Harper is soon caught up in a plot that involves Iris's sultry daughter, corrupt cops, a suspicious grounds keeper, an oil tycoon and an old millionairess.

The film was directed by Stuart Rosenberg and starred Paul Newman (below), Joanne Woodward (below), Melanie Griffith, Anthony Franciosa and Richard Jaeckl.

Oaklawn Manor served as the home of Iris Devereaux

OAKLEY PLANTATION
West Feliciana Parish

Construction on the Oakley Plantation house began in 1799, when Ruffin Gray, a successful planter from Natchez, Mississippi, moved here on land purchased from the Spanish authorities. Gray died before the house was completed, and his widow Lucy Alston oversaw its completion. She later married James Pierre of Scotland, a millwright who could very well have designed and built this remarkable structure.

Eliza, the daughter of James Pierre and Lucy, was born here in 1805, and it was her future education that introduced aspiring naturalist John James Audubon to the Felicianas.

Arriving at Oakley Plantation on June 18, 1821, Audubon wrote: "The rich magnolias covered with fragrant blossoms, the holly, the beech, the tall yellow poplar, the hilly ground and even the red clay, all excited my admiration." Audubon's stay at Oakley lasted only four months, but he painted 32 of his famous bird pictures here and developed a love for the beautiful West Feliciana Parish.

Mrs. Lucy Pierre brought the young Audubon to Oakley as a tutor for Eliza. The arrangement required that Audubon spend half his time teaching drawing to Eliza, but he was otherwise free to roam the woods and work on his naturalistic paintings. For this Audubon was to receive 60 dollars a month plus room and board for himself and his 13-year-old pupil assistant, John Mason. Audubon returned at a later date to join his wife, then teaching there, and his son.

When Oakley was built, it displayed state of the art architectural influences that had been developed in the West Indies to allow for better ventilation and air flow during the hot summers. The jalousied galleries (jalousies are wooden shutters) allowed cooling breezes to flow through, while blocking out some of the heat and direct sunlight of the day.

Oakley's interior has been restored to the Federal period style (1790-1830), reflecting its appearance when Audubon stayed here. The three-story home expresses the colonial architecture adapted to the geographical location. Oakley Plantation House contains 17 rooms, with front and side entrances leading to the landscaped grounds, which are shaded by oak and ancient crape myrtle trees.

Eliza's family did not approve of her first husband, Robert Barrow, a familiar rift between an old family and "new money," and perhaps due also to politics. Robert's father was a leader of the "successful rebellion against Spain in 1810 which had cost James Pierre his title of Alcaulde."

Eliza eloped to marry Robert in Natchez. After the couple had walked about in a rainstorm, however, Barrow contracted pneumonia and died. Eliza returned to Oakley to face her parents, eventually giving birth in 1824 to her son, Robert Hilliard Barrow. At that point she lived with her husband's family, the Barrows.

Her second husband, the Rev. William Bowman of Philadelphia, arrived in St. Francisville in 1827 to found Grace Episcopal Church, a wooden structure that eventually burned and which the present-day brick structure replaces. The union produced two children, one of whom, James P. Bowman, married Sarah Turnbull, the heiress of Rosedown, a marriage that produced 10 children.

The couple's daughter, Isabelle Bowman, married William Wilson Matthews and bought Oakley from her stepfather, Henry Lyons. Isabelle and William Matthews had six children, among them daughters Lucy and Ida Matthews who inherited Oakley. In 1947 the State of Louisiana acquired Oakley for use as an historic site.

Oakley Plantation was featured in several films.

Desire in the Dust - 1960

Raymond Burr stars as an aristocratic land-holder and prospective governor of a southern state. He portrays the tragic yet devil-may-care character of a man who has seen his youngest son die in an automobile accident, his daughter grow into a beautiful but immoral woman, his other son courting one of his tenant farmers and his wife become an invalid.

Desire in the Dust was produced and directed by William Claxton (right) and starred Burr, Martha Hyer and Ken Scott.

It was filmed totally on location in Louisiana, including scenes from Oakley Plantation. Other locations included Asphodel Plantation, Baton Rouge, Clinton and Zachery. According to various reports, both Burr and Claxton raved over the scenic beauty of the country-side, and the warm hospitality of the people.

Image below shows Burr in front of Clinton Courthouse.

Governor Jim Davis hosted a guest roster of luminaries when the film opened at its world premiere in Baton Rouge. The festivities began with a mammoth parade. The Baton Rouge mayor proclaimed September 15, 1960 "Desire in the Dust Day."

A Summer of the Birds - 2010

A Summer of Birds details a relatively unknown chapter in the life of renowned naturalist painter, ornithologist and literary figure John James Audubon.

Based on the acclaimed book, the documentary chronicles the formative summer Audubon spent in Louisiana in 1821, in the lush surroundings of Oakley Plantation in West Feliciana Parish. There, Audubon began or completed nearly half of the 435 pictures in his famous "Birds of America" collection.

Narrated by Emmy-winning actress Sela Ward, the film explores the profound influence of Louisiana's natural environment and birdlife on Audubon's development as an artist and writer, and conversely, Audubon's undeniable impact on the region and its cultural identity.

Cameras accompany modern-day birding enthusiasts and naturalists through Louisiana's bayous and woodsy pathways to experience their "paradise of birds" the same way Audubon did nearly 200 years ago.

The documentary was produced by Louisiana Public Broadcasting/Louisiana Educational Television Authority and filmed on location at Oakley Plantation.

RAMSAY PLANTATION
Point Coupee Parish

Ramsey Plantation is located on the banks of False River in Pointe Coupee Parish. The history of the plantation and details of the building campaigns are obscure. At one point, the plantation was known as the New Oliva House. It was build by Joseph Richy for Sidney Arnaud Lacoste and his wife, Victoire Virginie Esneault, in the middle of the nineteenth century. The name of the plantation was probably a corruption of "Olivet," one of the earliest owners, who bought the place from a Spanish official and obtained complete title in 1791. It was destroyed by a fire in 1860.

Set back behind a Cherokee rose hedge, it was a one-and-one-half story frame house. Square vine-clad plaster brick pillars support a gallery which extends around three sides and is reached by two outside stairways. The plantation was inherited by Victoire Virginie Esneault from her great aunt, Magdeleine Oliveau, wife of Simon Porche.

In 1853, a petition was filed with the District Court of the Ninth Judicial District of the State of Louisiana, in and for the Parish of Pointe Coupée. In that petition, Jean B. Bellocq of New Orleans presented to the court that he held a promissory note in the sum of $15,197.76, subscribed in 1847 by the late Magdeleine Oliveau, widow of the late Simon Porche, to Dr. Auguste Ferrier. The debt was secured by a "special mortgage" on Mrs. Porche's plantation located on a tract of land of eighteen "arpents" front by eighty in depth on False River in the parish of Pointe Coupée.

Two years later, Mrs. Porche sold a portion of her mortgaged plantation to a free woman of color named Cecile. She died some time later, leaving the debt and the remainder of her mortgaged plantation to her "universal legatee," Victoire Virginie Esnault, widow of Lacoste, but bequeathing a small tract of land in "usufruct" to Cecile. That bequest was contested by Mrs. Lacoste.

After Mrs. Porche's death, Dr. Auguste Ferrier obtained a judgment against Mrs. Lacoste, forcing her to buy the mortgaged plantation and sell some slaves to pay the inherited unpaid debt. With a little over $5,000 remaining unpaid, Jean B. Bellocq bought the note and the rights to the special mortgage from Dr. Ferrier. He then sued Mrs. Lacoste and her husband, as well as Cecile, to recover the balance of the debt.

Lt. Allan Ramsey Wurtele, who developed a machine harvester for sugar cane processing, purchased the 5,000 acre property in 1928. Wurtele granted the Josephite Fathers permission to use a building on the property as St. Catherine's Chapel in 1938. The home was rebuilt and named Ramsey. His daughter, Joanna Wurtele, owned the plantation as late as 2004. Ramsey serves as a private residence.

Ramsey is a raised Creole house with a few neoclassical details. The house is made of brick on the first floor, is framed on the second, and features a raised basement and spiral staircase in the hallway.

In 1958, the movie *Long Hot Summer* was filmed on location at Ramsey.

Long Hot Summer - 1958

This film is based in part on three short stories by William Faulkner.   Ben Quick is an ambitious drifter who arrives in Frenchman's Bend, MS after being kicked out of another town for allegedly burning a barn for revenge. When he is hired by Will Varner, the owner of most of the town, it sets off a series of conflicts within the Varner family.

The film starred Paul Newman (right), Joanne Woodward (right) and Orson Welles. It was directed by Martin Ritt.

ROSEDOWN PLANTATION
West Feliciana Parish

The parents of Daniel and Martha Hilliard Barrow Turnbull (below) achieved high social status in West Feliciana through their immense cotton operations. Daniel Turnbull was known before the Civil War as one of the richest men in the nation.

The land that became Rosedown Plantation, named for a play that the Turnbulls saw on their honeymoon, was assembled not by the then-usual method of Spanish Land Grants, but in a group of seven purchases made by Daniel Turnbull from the 1820s through the 1840s.

Daniel and Martha Turnbull began construction on the main house at Rosedown in November 1834. The house was constructed using cypress and cedar. Daniel had an onsite sawmill and a slave workforce of about 450 responsible for building the house at so little expense. In just six months, at a cost of over $13,000, the house was completed in the spring 1834.

The Federal-Greek revival style great house, complete with Grecian style wings (circa1845), is at the head of a 660-foot long oak allee. It is typical of the small minority of great houses built by the South's wealthiest planters. Near the great house are several dependencies, most notably three latticed summerhouses and a Greek temple style doctor's office.

The home was furnished with the finest pieces available, most imported from the North and from Europe. A surprising amount of the furnishings purchased by the Turnbulls remained with the house during the years after the Civil War and many original pieces are still on display at Rosedown.

The gardens were the passion of Martha Turnbull and her garden diary provides invaluable insight into the story of the garden's planting and management. She recorded her first entry in 1836 and her last in 1895, a year before her death at the age of 87. Eighteen acres of ornamental pleasure gardens illustrate a combination of the axiality of the Baroque style and the winding paths of the picturesque tradition. Many of the plants introduced by Martha survive today, and include one of the earliest collections of camellias in the Deep South. She also relied heavily on plants imported from the Orient, such as cryptomeria, azaleas and crape myrtles.

Daniel and Martha had three children at Rosedown: William, Sarah (left) and James Daniel. They would unfortunately lose both of their sons. Their youngest son, James Daniel, died at age 7 from yellow fever. Their eldest son, William, though he did marry and have 2 sons of his own, died at age 27 in a boating accident while crossing the Old River. This left their daughter Sarah as their only remaining heir.

In 1857, at the age of 26, Sarah married a local boy, James P. Bowman from the nearby Oakley Plantation. Since Sarah and James would be inheriting Rosedown, they moved into the mansion following their wedding.

The family continued to live at Rosedown Plantation during the Civil War, despite the massive siege and battle that took place just a short distance away at Port Hudson. Daniel Turnbull died in 1862, but family members continued to occupy the house.

The Bowmans had 10 children—8 girls and 2 boys. Of these 8 daughters, 4 would never marry. Sarah and James were very concerned about the futures of their unmarried daughters, so they decided to leave Rosedown to those four daughters. The last of these daughters died in1955, at which time the plantation was placed up for sale.

In 1956, Milton and Catherine Fondren Underwood of Houston, Texas purchased Rosedown. Catherine (left), an enthusiastic amateur horticulturalist, began an eight-year historic restoration of the house and formal gardens. Catherine was an oil heiress and spent approximately $10 million on this project.

The emphasis on restoration rather than renovation was applied to the formal gardens as well, which were reconstructed by Ralph Ellis Gunn using Martha Turnbull's extensive garden diaries. When possible, the same species and varieties were replanted. When plants in Martha's inventory were discovered to be no longer available, the staff of gardeners would propagate them from plant stock surviving in the gardens. Through this process, the gardens, as well as the house, were returned to their original state.

Catherine and Milton opened Rosedown to the public in 1964 and the Underwood family maintained Rosedown as a tourist site until 1994, when it was sold by their son David, to a businessman from Georgia. The Georgia owner sold it to the state of Louisiana in the year 2000.

Currently, the main house, historic gardens, 13 historic buildings and 371 remaining acres of Rosedown Plantation are preserved as a state historic site by the Office of State Parks. State Parks staff and volunteers work to conserve and maintain the site, conducting tours and programs to illustrate plantation life in the 1800s. In 2005, Rosedown Plantation was placed on the National Listing of Historic Landmarks.

Jonah Hex - 2010

Jonah Hex is a scarred drifter and bounty hunter of last resort, a stoic, battle-hardened gunslinger who can track down anyone...and anything. Having survived death, Jonah's violent history is steeped in myth and legend, and has left him with one foot in the natural world and one on the "other side." A man fated to wander alone, his sole human connection is with Lilah, whose life in a brothel has left her with scars of her own. Jonah's past is about to catch up with him when the U.S. military makes him an offer he can't refuse: in exchange for freedom from the warrants on his head, he must track down and stop the sinister terrorist Quentin Turnbull, the man who killed Hex's family and mutilated his face with a branding iron.

According to the film's production notes, the New Orleans area offered the production a wealth of divergent settings, beginning with the historic French Quarter, which only required a layering of dirt over the street, signage, horse drawn carriages and set dressing to look as it might have in the 1800s; the historic Rosedown Plantation in St. Francisville; City Park, a former golf course that became overgrown post-Hurricane Katrina, which became a town called Cactus Hole, complete with the narrow alleys of low slung adobe buildings and a fully built Catholic mission church with four-story bell tower co-opted into Lilah's brothel lording over the town; and Crown Point, on the edge of the Jean Lafitte Preserve. Another key location was historic Fort Pike, which is one of the only standing forts left from the early 19th century. Relatively unscathed from the war (though it did not escape Hurricane Katrina), it became Fort Resurrection' and they built 500 feet of full-scale running train cars at Raceland.

The film stars Josh Brolin (below) John Malkovich, Megan Fox, Michael Fassbender, Will Arnett and Aidan Quinn. Jimmy Hayward (below) directed the film.

THE SHADES
East Feliciana Parish

The Shades a/k/a Scott House or Scott Plantation was built by William Rochelle, Jr. for Alexander Scott in 1808 on a land grant. Scott had established the plantation in 1796 after he moved to Louisiana from Black Mino, South Carolina. His English heritage is reflected in the building of The Shades.

The two-story red brick home resembles a Carolina 'I" House, distinguished by a wide gallery on the first floor and chimneys at each end. Doric columns, an Adams mantel and twelve-pane windows are key features. Bordering the brick walk leading to the entrance is tall boxwood, and ivy twines its way around the thick porch columns. The kitchen, a main wing of the home, is built flush with the ground, its porches enclosed by narrow columns.

Scott's son, Major Gustavus Adolphus Scott, inherited the house, followed by his granddaughter Eva Scott (right). Eva lived on the plantation with her aunt, Kate Scott and uncle, Gus Scott. The Shades stayed within the Scott family until Eva's death. In 1994, George and Edrye Berger became the owners of The Shades.

Scenes for the ***The Undefeated*** were shot on location at The Shades.

The Undefeated - **1969**

In Louisiana, Confederate Colonel James Langdon, unwilling to accept life in a conquered land, leaves his once noble plantation in flames and departs for Mexico with his wife; daughter; and a party of about a hundred men, women and children. Travelling inconspicuously, the group evades interception by Union troops and crosses the Rio Grande into Mexico where they break out their Confederate flags and uniforms.

The film was directed by Andrew V. McLaglen and starred John Wayne, Rock Hudson, Lee Meriwether, Roman Gabriel and Merlin Olsen.

The Shades served as Colonel Langdon's plantation home Langdon Hall (2 scenes below)

SHADOWS-ON-THE-TECHE
Iberia Parish

In 1825, David Weeks and his wife Mary Clara Conrad Weeks (right) built Shadows-on-the-Teche on a tract of 158 acres. Construction of the new house began in 1831 and was finally completed in 1834. Invoices indicate that two brothers were in charge of most of the building process, Jotham and James Bedell.

One of only three brick structures on the bayou in New Iberia in the 1830s, the Shadows was constructed in a Classical Revival style on the exterior with the distinctive eight white columns across the front facade. Unlike other southern plantation homes of its time, the new Weeks home incorporated a Louisiana Colonial floorplan.

As the house neared completion in May 1834, David Weeks left on a sea voyage to New Haven, Connecticut, in an attempt to find a cure for a recurring unidentified disease. In mid-June 1834, Mary and six children moved into the new house. The happiness of moving into the new home was overshadowed by worry about the absent David Weeks, who died August 25, 1834, never having lived in the new house on Bayou Teche. The plantation was occupied by Union soldiers during the Civil War. Mary's refusal to abandon her home during the war probably saved it from confiscation and greater damage.

Four generations of the Weeks family lived at The Shadows from 1834 until 1958. The last owner was William Weeks Hall an accomplished artist (left).

After his father's death, Weeks Hall lived with his mother in New Orleans. He won several scholarships to study at the Pennsylvania Academy of the Fine Arts in Philadelphia, which he attended from 1913 to 1918. There he won additional scholarships to study in Europe, which he deferred due to World War I, until 1920 to 1922, when he studied in Paris and London.

Upon completion of his studies, Weeks returned to his family home in New Iberia, which was then called The Shadows-on-the-Teche after the Bayou Teche which borders the rear of the property. In 1919, Weeks Hall purchased his aunt's, Harriet Weeks Torian of New Orleans, half ownership of the homestead for $7,500, and he became its sole owner at the age of 25.

Weeks restored his home and created the magnificent gardens surrounding the property. Weeks tried to allay the growing progress surrounding his home by incorporating into the gardens a bamboo hedge around the skirt of the property.

He also attempted to prevent the "Path of Progress" by finding a suitable national agency to which he could bequeath the house, certain that it would be preserved for future generations. He contacted various organizations, including the National Park Service, to no avail.

Finally he sought out the company of the wealthy and famous of his day and invited them to visit his home. Visitors included artists, writers, and filmmakers such as Henry Miller, Lyle Saxon, Cecil B. DeMille, Emily Post, D.W. Griffith and Walt Disney. All were impressed with what he had done to preserve the house, enthralled with the setting he created, and charmed by his captivating personality.

In 1958 shortly before Hall's death, the National Trust for Historic Preservation accepted the home and property he bequeathed them for preservation and opened the site to the public in 1961.

D. W. Griffin was so impressed with Shadows-on-the-Teche that he filmed his 1923 movie **White Rose** on location at the plantation. In 1958, Cecil B. DeMille brought his production of **The Buccaneer** to film some historic scenes for the film.

White Rose - 1923

A wealthy young Southern aristocrat, Joseph Beaugarde, graduates from a seminary and, before he takes charge of his assigned parish, decides to go out and see what "the real world" is all about. He winds up in New Orleans and finds himself attracted to a poor, unsophisticated orphan girl who works at a cigar stand.

One thing leads to another, and before long Bessie finds that she is pregnant with Joseph's child. A remorseful Beaugarde returns to his Bayou Teche plantation to prepare for his ordination and his forthcoming marriage to Marie Carrington, a girl of his own social standing.

D. W. Griffith (right) directed the film, which starred Mae Marsh (below), Ivor Novello, Carol Dempster and Neil Hamilton.

Shadows-on-the-Teche served as the Beaugarde family's Bayou Teche plantation (below)

The Buccaneer - 1958

In 1958, famed pirate Jean Lafitte once again came to life on the silver screen. The 1958 film *The Buccaneer* was a remake of Cecille B. DeMille's 1938 Paramount production of the same title, also about Lafitte. The film took place during the War of 1812 and deals with the attempt of the British to capture New Orleans.

This 1958 DeMille version starred Yul Brynner (below), Charlton Heston, Claire Bloom, Charles Boyer, Inger Stevens, Henry Hull, E. G. Marshall and Lorne Green. An ailing DeMille turned to his son-in-law, Anthony Quinn (below), for the directing duties.

The Buccaneer made its world premiere in New Orleans as a benefit for the Louisiana Landmark Society, which was seeking to purchase the approximately sixty acres where the Battle of New Orleans was fought and preserve it as a national monument. The film did manage to make an impression on historians. Brynner's Jean Lafitte and Heston's Andrew Jackson were fairly accurate, according to some scholars (despite Heston's wig being much too white for the younger Jackson at this stage in his life). Sean Wilentz wrote in the book *Past Imperfect: History According to the Movies* that in emphasizing the importance of the New Orleans battle, *The Buccaneer* is "actually more trustworthy than many standard history textbooks."

Location shooting was done around New Orleans as well as the Shadows-on-the-Teche Plantation in New Iberia.

ST. JOSEPH PLANTATION

St. Joseph was built in the 1830s by Louis R. Scioneaux. The plantation, initially known as the Priestly House, was the residence of William Priestly, son of Joseph Priestly, the Unitarian minister and discoverer of oxygen.

The plantation's most famous son is Henry Hobson Richardson (right), Joseph Priestly's great grandson. Richardson was one of the nation's premier architects of the 19th century. He was born at St. Joseph Plantation in 1838. Richardson is renowned for designing the original Marshall Field store in Chicago and the Trinity Church of Boston, referred to by modern architects as being built in the "Richardsonian Romanesque" style.

In 1842, the house was sold to Dr. Cazimir Bernard Mericq, a French doctor who had served in Napoleon's army, and his wife Celeste Palyre Gauthier of Natchitoches. Dr. Mericq had been hired to care for the plantation masters, their families, and slaves. After his death in 1855, his widow sold the house and property to Gabriel Valcour Aime. Aime was known as the "Louis the XIV of Louisiana" and was reputedly the wealthiest man in the South. Aime gave it to his daughter Josephine and her husband Alexis Ferry II as a wedding gift.

The 12,000-square-foot antebellum plantation was constructed in a Raised Creole style that predates some of the nearby plantations which are Greek Revival style. Wide porches overlook the 1,000 acre property that is still farmed for sugar cane.

The house originally consisted of a large ballroom and four adjoining rooms. In 1858, Josephine and Alexis remodeled the house with Classical Revival elements and added four rooms and enclosed the ground floor to create a basement, where the open space had previously sheltered the horse-drawn buggy that Mericq used to visit his rural patients.

A storm devastated the property in 1866. This, coupled with reversals from the Civil War, led to the loss of the Ferry's fortune. In 1877, the plantation was sold in a sheriff's sale to Edward Gay, who immediately sold it to Joseph Waguespack.

Waguespack's purchase began a timeline of family ownership that has continued unbroken to this day. His descendants have traveled from all over the country to lovingly restore St. Joseph Plantation and its outbuildings. In 1901, Saturnine Waguespack merged St. Joseph Plantation with Felicity Plantation to form the St. Joseph Plantation and Manufacturing Company. It is today maintained by descendants of the Waguespack and Simon families.

According to the Live Oak Society of Louisiana, the company has 16 registered live oak trees on its property, some named after family members, with the largest boasting a girth of 23 feet. Officials estimate the trees are about 300 years old.

The St. Joseph Plantation was featured in the 1991 made-for-cable *Grand Isle*.

Grand Isle - 1991

Set in 19th-century Louisiana, the made-for-cable film *The Grand Isle* is about a wealthy married woman who meets and falls in love with a handsome Creole artist vacationing on Grand Isle, a resort on the Gulf of Mexico. When her affair changes her view of her life as a socialite, she tries to break away from her husband, resulting in a tragic end.

The film is based on the novel The Awakening by Kate Chopin, first published in 1899.

Grand Isle was directed by Mary Lambert and starred Kelly McGillis (right), Jon DeVries as Léonce Pontellier and Adrian Pasdar (right).

Scenes for *Grand Isle* were filmed on location at St. Joseph Plantation.

St. Louis Plantation
Iberville Parish

St. Louis Plantation home was built in 1857 by U.S. Rep. Edward J. Gay (right). Gay was born in Liberty, Bedford County, Va. The family moved west to Illinois then settled in St. Louis, Mo. Gay married Lavinia Hynes of Nashville in that city in 1840. It was his marriage to Lavinia that brought Gay to Louisiana. She was the daughter of Anne Erwin Hynes and Andrew Hynes, a Nashville merchant who acquired an interest in his father-in-law's plantation, Home, located in Iberville Parish near Plaquemine, in 1836.

When Andrew Hynes died in 1849, he owned one of the largest sugar plantations in Iberville Parish and 223 slaves valued at $86,000. Gay, acting as administrator of the Hynes estate, took over the management of Home Plantation. About 1856, after having purchased the interests of the other, Gay built a new residence at Home and changed the name of the plantation to St. Louis.

St. Louis Plantation has six columns and a gallery across the front, along with a rooftop belvedere. The home also has a cellar, which is quite rare among plantations. It is listed on the National Register of Historic Places.

During the Civil War, Edward J. Gay and his family remained for the most part at their Louisiana plantation, and he continued to engage in the purchase and sale of sugar and cotton.

After the war, Gay expanded his financial interests through the purchase of a partnership in the William Edwards and Company, a New Orleans factor house, and the acquisition of additional plantations by sales and foreclosures of mortgages. By 1868, Edward J. Gay either owned or was financially interested in St. Louis, Olivia, Keep, Mount Magnolia, Greenfield, Kleinpeter, and Oaks plantations located in Iberville and West Baton Rouge Parishes. The home is still in the control of the Gay family.

In 2010, St. Louis Plantation appeared in *Loss of a Teardrop Diamond*, the first time the home had appeared in a film.

Loss of a Teardrop Diamond - 2007

The Loss of a Teardrop Diamond is based on a recently rediscovered original screenplay by legendary writer Tennessee Williams. Set in the roaring twenties in the town of Memphis, the film tells the story of Fisher Willow. The headstrong young heiress chafes under the constraints of proper southern society, and rebels by asking the impoverished but handsome son of her father's caretaker, Jimmy Dobyne, to escort her to the major social events of the season.

The relationship is purely a business arrangement at the outset, with Fisher paying for Jimmy's time and attention, When she discovers that she really loves him, she finds it impossible to re-write the rules and earn the affection she tried to buy. The film starred Bryce Dallas Howard, Chris Evans, Ellen Burstyn, Ann-Margret, Mamie Gummer, and Will Patton. It was directed by Jodie Markell in her feature debut.

The Loss of a Teardrop Diamond was filmed around Louisiana including St. Louis Plantation (below); Nottoway Plantation; Greenwood Plantation; Houmas House; the gardens of Afton Villa Plantation, the Old Governor's Mansion and the Hotel Bentley.

LAGNIAPPE

Here are other plantations, estates and private homes that have been the backdrop for movies filmed on location in Louisiana.

COOK-TAYLOR HOUSE
Natchitoches, Louisiana

The Cook-Taylor house was originally built in the 1840's by Italian architects Trizini and Soldini for Louis Dupleix as a store. During the Civil War, it was used as a hospital. In the early 1900's, Jackson L. Bryan moved the home from its original location next to the sidewalk to where it now stands.

The round columns made of pie-shaped bricks were carefully removed. The original bricks were used in the rebuilding process and the architectural design basically was preserved. "Pilgrim's Rest", a name given it by the Bryan family, was sold to the family of Herman Taylor, Sr. in the early 1940s.

The four story home, including cellar and attic, was restored and modernized to fit needs of a family of three boys. Grillwork, brick posts, veranda and family room were added, and eight fireplaces were closed and replaced with gas logs.

In 2003, Karen and Paul Rinehart purchased the home and transformed it into the Steel Magnolia House Bed and Breakfast. Christina Landry, the current owner, planned to convert the house back into a residence, but continued to run it as a bed & breakfast when she found she really enjoyed meeting the guests.

The house was put up for auction in October, 2013.

Cook-Taylor House is now known as "The Steel Magnolias House" as it was the location of the film of the same name.

Steel Magnolias - 1989

Steel Magnolias focuses on the bond among a group of women from a fictional parish in the Natchitoches area. It was based on the 1987 play *Steel Magnolias* which was written by Robert Harling, a native of the area. The play and film were based on the death of Harling's younger sister, Susan Harling Robinson, a diabetic.

Steel Magnolias was directed by Herbert Ross and starred Sally Field, Shirley MacLaine, Olympia Dukakis, Dolly Parton, Daryl Hannah and Julia Roberts (Image below: bottom left to right: MacLaine, Dukakis; Roberts. Top left to right: Parton, Fields, Hannah).

The Cook-Taylor House served as the Eatonton residence. Most of the interior house scenes were filmed inside the house. Outside shots included the front of the house and the backyard.

FLEMING CEMETERY
Barataria, Louisiana

Fleming (a/k/a Berthoud) Cemetery is located on a large Indian mound on the banks of Bayou Barataria in the community of Barataria. Tombs and graves are located along the sides and around the base of a large Indian mound, approximately 12 feet high and 50 feet in diameter. The cemetery was named after the Berthoud brothers, one of whom was a nineteenth century owner of the Mavis Grove Plantation, within which the mound was located and for which it probably served as a plantation burial ground. The brothers are buried at the top of the mound.

This cemetery was used as the opening scene of the 1955 film *Pete Kelly's Blues*.

Pete Kelly's Blues- 1955

Pete Kelly's Blues is based on the 1951 original radio series. In the film Pete Kelly fronts a seven-man jazz band in a Kansas City speakeasy in 1927. When a local racketeer attempts to extort 25% of the band's fees, Kelly agrees, much to the chagrin of his band. However, when his drummer is later killed, Kelly fights back.

The film starred Jack Webb, Janet Leigh, Lee Marvin and Edmond O'Brien. It was directed by Webb.

Webb went to New Orleans to film the opening pre-credit sequence, the funeral of a black jazz musician against the slow passage of a riverboat in 1915. The dead man's silver cornet falls off the horse-drawn funeral wagon and surfaces in the next sequence in Jersey City, 1919, where Webb's demobilized WW I doughboy wins it in a boxcar crap game. This scene was shot on location at Fleming Cemetery (right).

MACDONELL PLANTATION
Lake Arthur, Louisiana

John Revlon, a wealthy Creole from New Orleans, built the MacDonell Plantation in 1855. The plantation was acquired by John Angus "Rice King" MacDonell and Frances "Aunt Frank" MacDonald MacDonell. The MacDonell Plantation was famous for production of rice, cotton, citrus fruit, and live stock.

The John Sayles' movie *Passion Fish* was filmed on site in 1992.

Passion Fish - 1992

Indie director John Sayles (right) captured the many layers of conflict in the Louisiana bayou country of race, class, and country -versus-city in **Passion Fish**, a thoughtful and funny character drama released in 1992.
The story revolved around a New York City actress' return to her family's country home after a paralyzing accident and her relationship with her nurse.

The film starred Mary McDonnell, Angela Bassett, David Straitharn, Lenore Banks, and William Mahoney.

Filmed on location in Elton, Gueydan, Jennings, Lake Arthur and Lake Charles, the MacDonnell Plantation was prominently featured in the film.

FICTIONAL PLANTATIONS

When location shooting was either too costly or inconvenient, many filmmakers chose to capture the spirit of antebellum Louisiana by recreating elegant plantation sets at their studios. For example, the 1913 films **Octoroon** (below) and **White Slave** each took place on an unnamed Terrebonne Parish plantation. Other films set on Louisiana plantations during that period include **Cameo Kirby**, 1914; **Under Southern Skies**, 1915; and **Cameo Kirby**, 1923.

In 1938, director Robert Haas built a Louisiana plantation house on the Warner Bros. ranch for his film *Jezebel*, which starred Bette Davis and Henry Fonda (below)

While some location shooting was done in Louisiana by a second filming unit, the bulk of *Jezebel* was filmed at the Warner Brothers studio.

According to modern sources, location shooting was not considered since star Henry Fonda had an agreement with Warner Bros. that his work on the film would be finished by early December, 1937 so that he could attend the birth of his child [Jane Fonda] in the East. To ensure authenticity in all aspects of the film, Haas hired Dalton S. Reymond, who was at that time the head of the opera department at Louisiana State University (L.S.U.).

Way Down South, the 1939 pre-Civil War film was set on the fictional Bayou Lovelle Plantation.   In 1944, the studios created a plantation named Belleville for the psychological thriller **Dark Waters**, starring Merle Oberon.

By the 1950's, location shooting gained favor with studios and more filmmakers came to Louisiana to shoot their plantation-based films.

Some studios still opt to recreate the Louisiana sets in other locations. However, with the introduction of the tax credit act, Louisiana is now the number one place to shoot on location -- and the historically significant plantation homes of yesteryear are a major draw for movie makers

REFERENCES

Poole, E. and S. Poole. *Louisiana Film History: A Comprehensive Overview Beginning 1896.* Donaldsonville, LA: Margaret Media, Inc., 2012

Poole, E. and S. Poole. *Hollywood on the Bayou.* Gretna, LA: Learn About Network, L.L.C, 2011

WEBSITES:

Louisiana Digital Library - www.louisdl.louislibraries.org/

National Park Services - www.nps.gov

Afton Villa Plantation - www.aftonvilla.com

Ardoyne Plantation - www.ardoyneplantation.com

Asphodel Plantation - www.plantationvillagestudios.com

Bocage Plantation - www.bocageplantation.com

Destrehan Plantation - www.destrehanplantation.org

Evergreen Plantation - www.evergreenplantation.org

Goodwood Plantation - www.goodwoodmuseum.org

Greenwood Plantation - www.greenwoodplantation.com

Houmas House - www.houmashouse.com

Laura Plantation - www.lauraplantation.com

Madewood Plantation - www.madewood.com

Myrtles Plantation - www.myrtlesplantation.com

Nottoway Plantation - www.Nottoway.com

Oak Alley Plantation - www.oakalleyplantation.com

Shadows on the Teche - www.shadowsontheteche.com

St. Joseph Plantation - www.stjosephplantation.com

INDEX TO MOVIE TITLES

Made in the USA
San Bernardino, CA
17 June 2016